MEGALITH

BLOOMSBURY PUBLISHING
Bloomsbury Publishing Inc.
1385 Broadway, New York, NY 10018, USA

BLOOMSBURY, BLOOMSBURY PUBLISHING,
and the Diana logo are trademarks of
Bloomsbury Publishing Plc

MEGALITH
STUDIES IN STONE

BLOOMSBURY
NEW YORK · LONDON · OXFORD · NEW DELHI · SYDNEY

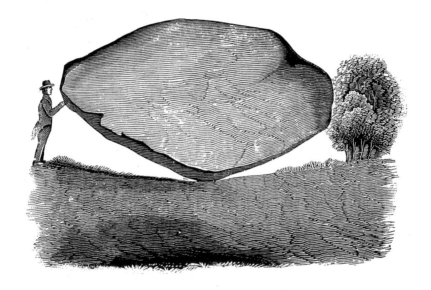

Rocking Stone at Fall River, Massachusetts;
woodcut by Orra White Hitchcock, 1840,
courtesy Amherst College Archives.

CONTENTS

Above: Niche in coralline limestone at Mnajdra South Temple, dated c.4000 BC, on the south coast of Malta, close to the vast Hagar Qim megalithic complex.

EDITOR'S PREFACE

We are not the first people to build in stone, and we will not be the last. All over Europe, indeed all over the world, long before the Romans, Greeks and ancient Egyptians, a much older civilisation was building stone temples whose remains still lie scattered across hills, plains and remote islands. At first glance these rough ruins can appear crude and inelegant, but look more closely and profound questions begin to surface, questions which remain unanswered today: Why build with such large stones? Why drag them so far? How were they moved? Why the fixation with the Sun, Moon and stars, and why the sophisticated geometry? In 2007, I started a conference, *Megalithomania*, with John Michell, Gareth Mills and Hugh Newman, to better frame and answer some of these questions.

This book is a compilation of material from seven books in the Wooden Books series. We begin with Hugh Newman's worldwide overview of *Stone Circles*. Next up is Howard Crowhurst's analysis of the world's most extensive megalith site, *Carnac*. Following this, Robin Heath tells the story and the secrets of *Stonehenge*. Then we tour *Avebury* with Evelyn Francis, explore *Stanton Drew* with Gordon Strong, and discover the remote site of *Callanish* with Gerald Ponting. We close with Chris Mansell's beautiful treatise on *Ancient British Rock Art* and twenty surveys of stone circles by the late Professor Alexander Thom.

The mysteries of the megaliths are profound, and puzzle all who take the time to ponder them ... what *were* the ancients up to?

John Martineau

Stone Circle, Jersey, Channel Islands. In 1785 these stones were removed and shipped 500 miles to General Henry Seymour Conway's garden near Henley-on-Thames, and placed in their original arrangement! From Old England: A Pictorial Museum of National Antiquities *by Charles Knight, 1844.*

STONE
CIRCLES

Hugh Newman

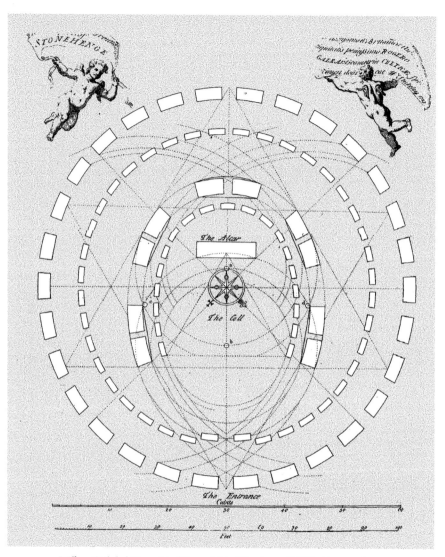

The Altar

The Cell

The Entrance

Cubits

Feet

William Stukeley's Geometrical Groundplot of Stonehenge. Published in 1740, this is
the first accurately imagined plan of the site as it would have stood before ruination.

INTRODUCTION

Stone circles conjure up a lost world of mysterious ceremonies, druid astronomers, pagan dances and inquisitive antiquarians. The most famous is Stonehenge in Wiltshire, UK, but it is also the most unusual in that it has *lintels* and *trilithons* in its design. Most stone circles are not so glamorous, but with over one thousand of them documented in the British Isles alone, dated between 3500 BC and 1500 BC, their construction was evidently an important part of our ancient culture.

Stonehenge is also well known for its summer solstice sunrise, and research over the last 60 years has shown that many other circles likewise use sky and landscape alignments to mark astronomical events, with many also sharing geometrical forms and measurement systems.

How such mighty rings were constructed has long baffled archaeologists, antiquarians, and other interested parties. In the 1600s, Christians often cited natural or supernatural explanations, and thus the devil, giants, witches and a host of mythological figures all crop up in local construction legends. For how else were such multi-ton stones quarried, transported and arranged with such precision? Avebury is so large that a village today sits within its main circle; its tallest stone was of such magnitude that, once broken up, an entire church could be constructed from it.

Whoever made these magnificent structures had a very deep understanding of engineering, surveying, geometry, metrology and astronomy. And they were not an isolated group of builders—as we will see in the pages which follow, stone circle building was once a truly global endeavour.

GÖBEKLI TEPE
stone circle genesis

6,500 years older than Stonehenge, 7,000 years before the pyramids of Egypt were constructed, predating the agricultural revolution, a vast megalithic complex sat atop the hills near present day Şanliurfa, southeast Turkey. Göbekli Tepe (*see opposite*) was flourishing an astonishing 12,000 years ago and its preserved stone circles (the oldest in the world thus far discovered, numbering as many as 60 across the site) exhibit impressive degrees of technical and artistic skill. They consist of T-shaped pillars up to 20 ft tall, many decorated with animal reliefs (scorpions, boars, lions, etc.) and abstract human forms wearing belts with enigmatic 'H' and 'U' shapes. The taller stones rest in shallow nests on bedrock with small supportive dry-stone walls built in between. In some enclosures two central pillars orient towards a holed stone, the largest and oldest is 65 ft wide. An enormous limestone pillar still sits in the nearby quarry, a staggering 24 ft long!

Over some 3,000 years the circles were filled in with rubble to create mounds, and other circular enclosures built on top. Then, around 8000 BC the entire complex was carefully reconstructed and covered up. Interestingly, the oldest rings are the biggest and most sophisticated.

Like later sites across the world, astronomical alignments are evident (*see opposite*). Figures depicted on the Vulture Stone may be the earliest representations of zodiacal and other constellations (including Cygnus) (*see opposite*). Our earliest surviving building seems to be an observatory, built to track precession, the 25,800-year cycle of the pole stars.

Unusual cup-marks on the bedrock and on top of some of the oldest pillars prefigure British cup-marks, thousands of years later.

Left: General plan of two enclosures at Göbekli Tepe with the two massive T-shaped pillars in the central areas, and the smaller pillars surrounding them in the retaining wall.

Above left: The "Vulture Stone," showing Cygnus and an orb. Above right: Plan of Göbekli Tepe's main enclosures showing their orientations (by Rodney Hale). The later Enclosure E aligns ENE or WSW, close to summer solstice sunrise or winter solstice sunset. The central pillars of Enclosure D align just west of north to Deneb, the brightest star of Cygnus at 9,400 BC. It orients through a holed stone.

THE NEOLITHIC EXPLOSION
the earliest megaliths

As we have just seen, Turkish stone circles were being constructed over 12,000 years ago. Elsewhere around the Mediterranean, other early sites testify to similar activity. ATLIT YAM, a submerged semi-circle off the coast of Israel, dates to 6900 BC (*see p. 55*), the earliest phase of the CROMLEQUE DOS ALMENDRES in Portugal (*see p. 49*) dates to 6000 BC, and KARAHUNGE (*see p. 55*) in Armenia goes back to 5500 BC.

Six and a half thousand years ago, what we now call *megalithic* structures begin to appear in Brittany, France and Britain (*megalith* means 'huge stone'). Ancient British tribes heaped earth upon dry-stone walled chambers to create tomb temples called *long barrows*. These enigmatic sites, such as the WEST KENNET LONG BARROW (*below*), date mostly from the early Neolithic, and predate the much grander constructions like those at Avebury, Silbury Hill and Stonehenge.

The earliest circles in the British Isles, the great boulder circles of Sligo (*see p. 44-45*), date to around 4600 BC, and monolithic rings then remained all the rage until around 1400 BC, when construction stopped.

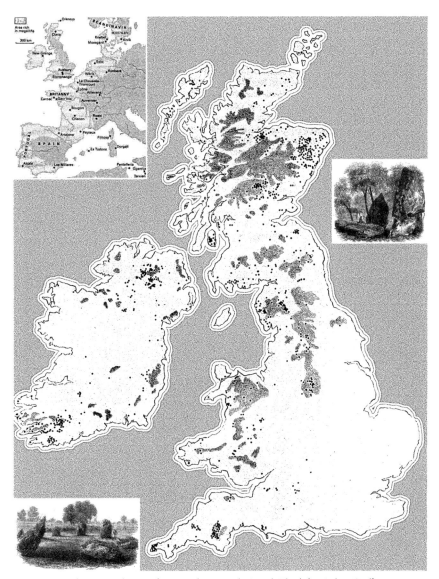

Above: Distribution of stone circles across the British Isles (after Aubrey Burl).

THE ANTIQUARIAN VIEW
some early ideas

The earliest phase of *megalithomania* in Britain was sparked by the English antiquary and writer John Aubrey [1626–1697]. Out hunting around Avebury, aged 22, he was deeply moved by the magnificent landscape temple laid out before him. This and other megalithic sites he visited, most notably Stonehenge (*see pp.20-21, & 123-187*) and the Rollright Stones (*see pp. 28-29*), are described in his *Monumenta Britannica*, curiously not published in its entirety until 1980. Previously, Inigo Jones [1573–1652] had declared that Stonehenge was built by the Romans and not the Druids, a notion that was not particularly popular (*see his illustration of the reconstructed Stonehenge below*).

The most famous antiquarian was Lincolnshire doctor-turned-clergyman William Stukeley [1687-1765], who traveled the English countryside, illustrating what he saw. He came to believe, like John Aubrey, that Druids were the original builders of these sites, saying of Stonehenge that 'it pleases like a magical spell'. Such theories stimulated the resurgence in modern Druidry that is still evident at Stonehenge and other sites today.

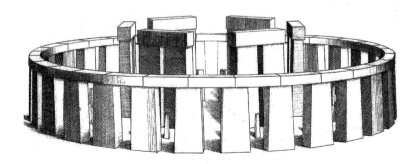

Above: 'The Cromlech at Trefigneth,' Anglesey. Near the shore, these dolmens are the remains of stone burial chambers (or barrows) after the outer layer of soil has been eroded or removed.

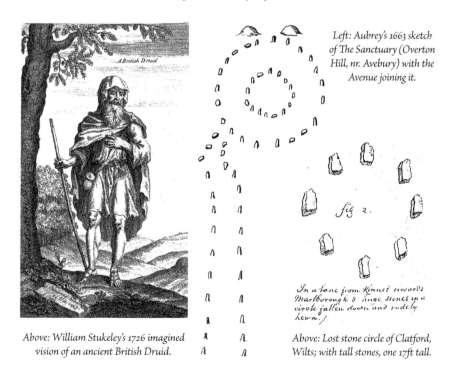

Left: Aubrey's 1663 sketch of The Sanctuary (Overton Hill, nr. Avebury) with the Avenue joining it.

Above: William Stukeley's 1726 imagined vision of an ancient British Druid.

Above: Lost stone circle of Clatford, Wilts; with tall stones, one 17ft tall.

CONSTRUCTION TECHNIQUES
hard labour or light work

So how did the ancients build their stone circles? In Geoffrey of Monmouth's 1150 *The History of the Kings of Britain*, a tantalizing legend states that Merlin, in constructing Stonehenge, used 'gears' to move stones from Ireland. The book also mentions giants, and the earliest known depiction of the site (*opposite*) depicts Merlin directing one moving a lintel into place. Unlike Stonehenge, which has beautifully cut stones, some from Preseli in Wales (100 miles away over difficult terrain), most circles are built from rough-hewn stones. However, they still had to be transported, aligned and set in place (*see Richard Atkinson's suggested techniques opposite, and Keith Critchlow's construction below*).

Mysteries remain. At Coral Castle in Florida, Edward Leedskalnin [1887–1951] single-handedly quarried, cut and raised massive blocks of coral, yet his methods remain unclear. In the 1960s John Michell [1933–2009] popularised ideas around the 'earth force'—*telluric* and magnetic currents that might levitate large stones. In the 1970s Paul Devereux [1945–] showed that many stone circles display peculiar electromagnetic and acoustic properties, especially at dawn and dusk.

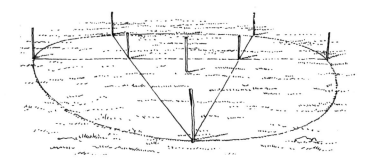

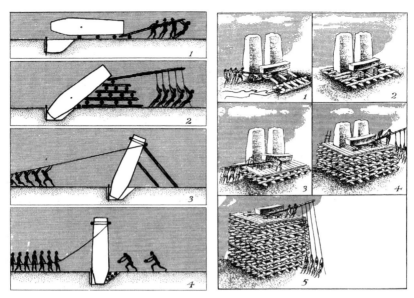

Above: Richard Atkinson's 1959 proposal for raising the Stonehenge sarsens and lintels.

Above left: A giant helps Merlin raise a lintel, from Le Roman de Brut *by the poet Wace, c. 1150.*
Above right: Artist's impression of tribal people moving a heavy stone on wooden rollers.

ARCHAEOASTRONOMY
celestial calculators & cosmic alignments

Discoveries in the 1880s by Alfred Lionel Lewis, and then by Sir Norman Lockyer [1836-1920] and Admiral Somerville [1882-1949], showed that many megalithic sites had astronomical alignments. Lockyer noted alignments within Stonehenge, including the summer solstice sunrise. Then, from 1957, Professor Alexander Thom [1894-1985] surveyed over 300 stone circles (*see pp.136-137 & 384-403*). In his words:

> *Sightlines were ranged from a point in the circle towards the Sun at the solstices, equinoxes and other feast days of the calendar, marked on the horizons by stone pillars, cairns or by natural features, such as peaks, notches in mountain ranges or distant islands.*

Thom discovered that the 18.61-year lunar cycle was encoded into many circle sites (*e.g. Callanish, p. 312*), and he also found strong parallels between sites in Brittany and the northern tip of Scotland.

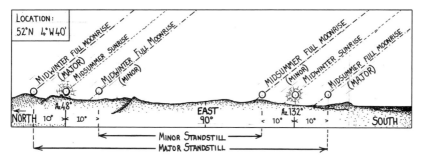

LOCATION:
52°N 4°W 40'

MIDWINTER FULL MOONRISE (MAJOR)
MIDSUMMER SUNRISE
MIDWINTER FULL MOONRISE (MINOR)
MIDSUMMER FULL MOONRISE (MINOR)
MIDWINTER SUNRISE
MIDSUMMER FULL MOONRISE (MAJOR)

NORTH 10° ← 10° →   EAST 90°   Az 48°   Az 132°   ← 10° ✳ 10° →   SOUTH

← MINOR STANDSTILL →
← MAJOR STANDSTILL →

Above: Over 18.6 years the Moon's extreme rising and setting positions oscillate each side of the sun's (from Sun, Moon and Earth, *by Robin Heath). Below left: Today's midsummer solstice sunrise alignment. Below right: Eightfold geometry at Stonehenge (after Gerald Hawkins & John Martineau).*

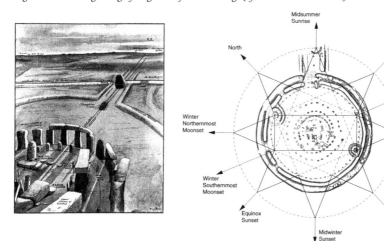

Midsummer
Sunrise

North

Equinox
Sunrise

Summer
Northernmost
Moonrise

Winter
Northernmost
Moonset

Summer
Southernmost
Moonrise

Winter
Southernmost
Moonset

Equinox
Sunset

South

Midwinter
Sunset

Left: "Nine Stones Close," Derbyshire. A little further south is the rock outcrop of Robin Hood's Stride which may have served as a sacred hill altar. From the centre of the circle the major southern moon is seen to set between the two stone pillars on top of the hill.

ALIGNMENTS AND LEYS
the ancient survey

In the 1920s Alfred Watkins [1855-1935] discovered interesting alignments between ancient sites, and ley-hunters soon found that most stone circles lie on a *ley*, their orientation often a clue to another site in the corresponding direction (*see the Silbury ley below*). Some leys stretch across the whole of Britain—the May Day sunrise St. Michael Line (*see opposite, top*) goes from Lands End to the Hurlers and on to Glastonbury, Avebury and Bury St Edmunds in the east. The mighty north-south Belinus Line connects many stone circles too. Is this merely a coincidence, or was there a great survey in prehistoric times?

The early mapping of Britain is something Alexander Thom pondered, for he had discovered a coherent system of geometry, metrology and astronomy across multiple sites. More recently, Robin Heath has proposed the existence of a great landscape Pythagorean triangle marking important points in the landscape across a large geographic area (*see opposite*). Stonehenge is also connected to Lundy Island and the Preseli Bluestone site in Wales (where an oval stone enclosure called BEDD ARTHUR or Arthur's Grave resides). In 2007, Heath, along with the author and some of the Leyhunters group, discovered a lost egg-shaped stone circle on Lundy Island, very close to the elbow of the 5-12-13 triangle. Other researchers have repeatedly found massive isosceles triangles connecting megalithic sites.

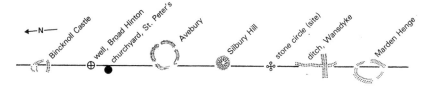

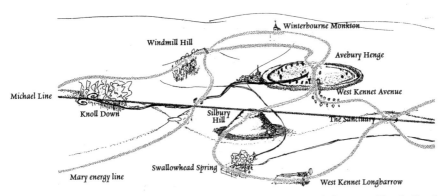

Above: Part of the great St. Michael line in the Avebury landscape with the proposed 'Michael' and 'Mary' earth-energy currents weaving in and around key sites (after Broadhurst and Miller).

Above: One of the many famous leys through Stonehenge.

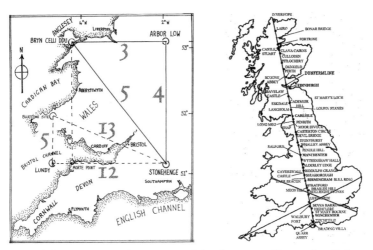

Above left: Two great triangles, one 3-4-5 and the other 5-12-13. These two huge Pythagorean landscape triangles both have corners at Stonehenge (after Robin Heath). Right: The Belinus Line.

WHY WERE THEY BUILT?

what a song and dance

We now know that thousands of people travelled from all over Britain to gather at Stonehenge and nearby Durrington Walls for the winter solstice to meet, feast, frolic, marry, dance, trade, share information and observe the heavens. Compacted earth within other rings supports other local folk memories of people dancing and celebrating. Is this why early Christians were so keen to control these sites and link them with the devil? Right up until 626 AD BOSCAWEN-UN in Cornwall had a reputation as a *gorsedd* (place of judgement), where tribal leaders settled legal matters and discussed astronomy and other sciences.

Many circles have acoustic properties that can enhance and relocate the human voice; some stones, when hit, reverberate. Were these used to affect human consciousness? MEN-AN-TOL (*below*), also in Cornwall, is said to cure sick infants. Research by John Burke suggests that the circle builders were interested in telluric currents and underground water as a way of 'charging' seeds and grains to increase yields. T.C. Lethbridge reported that he got an electric shock when he touched certain stones of the MERRY MAIDENS in Cornwall (*p. 22*). At Scorhill on Dartmoor (*p. 24*), horses were unwilling to ride through the stone circle, and there is a similar account from Avebury in 1823.

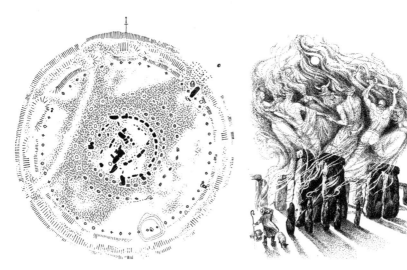

Above: Stonehenge ground resistivity plan, possibly showing telluric currents entering through the entrance.

Above: Mary Caine's "The Giant's Dance of Life and Power" - mystical Stonehenge.

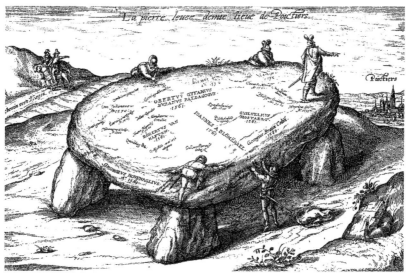

Above: French scholars study and ponder the PIERRE LEVÉE dolmen at Poitiers.

AVEBURY & STONEHENGE
the mightiest megalithic circles

Before we take a tour around the stone circles of Britain and beyond, let's remind ourselves of perhaps the two most important circle sites in the world—both located in Wiltshire.

The great 5,200-year-old AVEBURY henge took an estimated 1,560,000 man-hours and 4,000 people to construct. Over 200,000 tons of chalk was quarried and removed. This is before any of the 500 huge rough-hewn stones were bought from Fyfield Down (several miles away) and erected in the great circles, the AVENUE, and the SANCTUARY (*see opposite and pp. 191-245*). Other stone circles once existed within the Avebury landscape, and a second avenue (the BECKHAMPTON AVENUE) once ran from the western entrance of the henge. FAULKNER'S CIRCLE, dating to around 2500BC, is now just one stone in a hedge. The CLATFORD CIRCLE (*see p. 11*), sketched by John Aubrey, had 8 huge stones (one nearly 17ft tall) on 'a lane leading from Kennet to Marlborough.'

Originally known as 'The Giant's Dance', no other stone circle in the world has a design as sophisticated as STONEHENGE (*see pp. 123-187*). Like Avebury it has an avenue, which was lined with regularly spaced stones in Stukeley's day and may once have terminated at a stone circle on the banks of the River Avon in AMESBURY. Interestingly, three massive timber posts were erected at Stonehenge around 8000BC, but nothing further was constructed there until work began on the stone circle 5,000 years later. Excavations have shown that bluestones from the Preseli Mountains in Wales were used in its construction.

Despite its fame, Stukeley wrote that Avebury exceeds Stonehenge in greatness "as a Cathedral doeth a parish church".

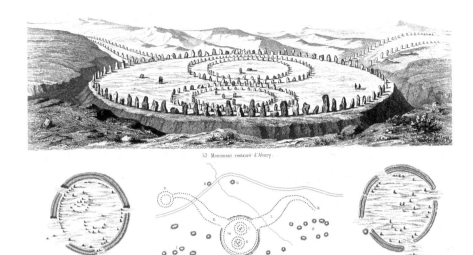

52. Monument restauré d'Abury.

54. Plan en 1722. 53. Plan général restauré. 55. Plan dans l'état actuel.

Above: 19th century French imaginative illustration of Avebury, showing the site as it stood in 1722 (left), as it stood in 1850 (right), and a full reconstruction (top). Engraving by J. Gailhabaud.

Above: Grand Conventional Festival of the Britons. An imaginative take on Stonehenge, 1815.

BODMIN & LAND'S END
triplets, alignments & lost circles

Cornwall is home to more megalithic sites per square mile than anywhere else in Britain. Seventeen circles remain, with many more lost or destroyed. On Bodmin Moor can be found THE HURLERS, three stones of 26-28 stones, with a recently excavated crystal pathway. The chunky white quartz DULOE CIRCLE is nearby, and the enormous STANNON CIRCLE and the TRIPPETT STONES all share this landscape.

Land's End has several rings of nineteen stones, possibly marking the 19-year Metonic cycle. BOSCAWEN-UN (*see opposite*) has 19 granite stones, one of quartz, which marks the Beltane (May 1st) sunrise from a central leaning pillar, while an outlier marks Samhain (November 1st). The perfectly circular MERRY MAIDENS near Penzance (*see below*) consists of 19 'dressed' granite stones; local legend states girls dancing on the sabbath were turned to stone. Two large menhirs called THE PIPERS sit a quarter of a mile north, and another pillar called GOON RITH to the west. Also in Land's End are the NINE MAIDENS circle of Boskednan and the TREGESEAL DANCING STONES circle near St. Just, the sole survivor of a complex set of stone circles (*opposite centre left*).

Above, with survey below centre: Two views of Boscawen-Un, Penzance, a Type-B flattened circle with Beltane and Samhain sunrise alignments. Lockyer believed it was one of the three 'Gorsedds' of Britain.

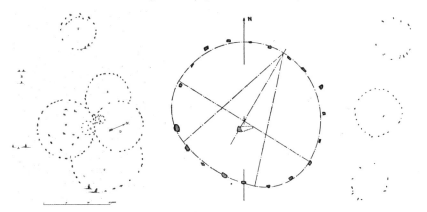

Left: A complex of stone circles near St. Just, now lost, as recorded by William Borlase in 1738. Centre: Type-B geometry of Boscawen-un. Right: The Hurlers triple circle, Bodmin Moor.

Facing page: The Merry Maidens stone circle in 1804. Above left: Illustration of the Nine Maidens in Cornwall by William Copeland Borlase, 1872. Right: The Pipers, two standing stones 13 ft and 15 ft tall.

Dartmoor & Exmoor
fairy rows & enchanted circles

Dartmoor is a rugged landscape of rocky tors, waterfalls and wild horses. It also has a rich megalithic heritage. Sixteen stone circles remain, with others dismantled or sunk below the marshy surface, including one discovered in 2009 under Tottiford reservoir. Over 60 stone rows (*see opposite*) have been recorded and many, such as Merrivale and Shovel Down, interact with adjacent rings. At Down Tor, a single row of 174 stones extends northeast from the stone circle.

To the east and south are several large open rings built during the later Neolithic. Scorhill (*below*) originally had around 70 stones, but only 34 remain with 25 still standing, the tallest at 8 ft. After 2300 BC, as the weather improved, smaller circles were constructed higher up, often with more stone rows. The Grey Wethers (*opposite, the only double circle on Dartmoor*) and Fernworthy Circle are fine examples.

Exmoor once had plenty of rings, but most are now gone, and those that remain have very small stones. Two survivors are Porlock and the huge Withypool. Porlock is 80 ft wide—of 43 original stones only 14 remain, and a nearby stone row. Withypool has 35 left (originally 100).

Above: The atmospheric stone rows of Dartmoor; single, double and triple variants remain.
Below: The Grey Wethers double stone circle on the edge of Fernworthy Forest, now restored.
Opposite page: Scorhill, described by Rev. Samuel Rowe as "by far the finest of the rude but venerable shrines of Druidical worship in Devonshire". 34 stones remain, 25 standing, tallest 8 ft.

SOUTHERN CIRCLES
lost, fallen & hidden

The 4,000-year-old remains of REMPTONE stone circle on the Isle of Purbeck were hidden for decades in woods, but their size suggests it was once a major ceremonial centre. Other notable Dorset circles include the oval shaped NINE STONES at Winterbourne Abbas (*opposite*), the 18 fallen stones of KINGSTON RUSSELL near Abbotsbury, and KING-BARROW (a.k.a. the Frolic, Easton Druid Temples, or Sawmill)—curiously hidden away in an old limekiln on Portland.

TISBURY in Wiltshire once had an impressive stone circle with a 12 ft central pillar, but it was transformed into a grotto for Old Wardour Castle in the 18th century. Around Avebury, numerous other rings were once evident, but no stones still stand save for one outlier at WINTERBOUNE BASSET. At TAN HILL in All Cannings there was once a tiny circle of nine 4ft stones, five remain fallen today. Another small circle, 16–20ft wide with eight recumbent stones was reported in 1923 at LANGDEAN BOTTOM in East Kennet. Close by was HARESTONE CIRCLE.

TWYFORD in Hampshire once had an important Bronze Age circle. Sadly the 'Druid Temple' was built over by a Saxon Church. When this was taken down in 1878, twelve menhirs were found in the foundations, and lie there still; other stones are scattered in the locale.

Kent is famous for the long barrows of the MEDWAY area, but a stone circle once graced the area just to the north. A map of 1869 shows it near the church of Mary Madgalene, but it is absent from later maps. The stones appear to have been redeployed as curbing along an area of green space nearby. Rediscovered by Mr. L. Peters in the 1990s, there are 19 of them, a soli-lunar number often found in Cornish circles.

Above: Stukeley's illustration of the Nine Stones (or Nine Ladies or Devil's Nine Stones), Dorset.
Right: Harestone circle, Wilts, with central pyramidal stone and Samhain sunset alignment.

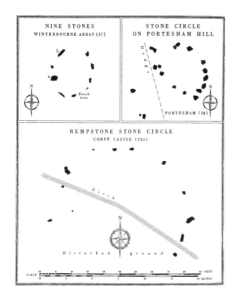

Above: Stukeley's 1724 sketch of the "Double circle of Stones" at Winterbourne Bassett, now mostly destroyed.

Left: A selection of surveys of stone circles in Dorset, published by Her Majesty's Stationery Office in the 1960s.

AVON TO SHROPSHIRE
rude rings in rough rock

STANTON DREW (*opposite top*) in N. Somerset is Britain's finest triple circle and the third most important overall. In 1723, William Stukeley noted an avenue extending from the main circle. The largest circle has a diameter of 368 ft (112 m). Only Avebury is larger.

At the ROLLRIGHT STONES (*opposite bottom*), a complex of three monuments on the Oxfordshire/Warwickshire border, there is one circle of 77 eroded limestone menhirs just over 100 ft wide called THE KING'S MEN. To the northeast is the KING STONE, which, strangely, is in a different county (Warwickshire). Four hundred yards southeast are the remains of the WHISPERING KNIGHTS dolmen.

Closer to Oxford is the 4,000-5,000 year-old DEVIL'S QUOIT, a huge stone circle recently fully restored to its former glory. Its stones and prominent henge can be seen in the image (*opposite centre right*).

Hugging the border with Wales are a few circles. Fifteen stones remain at MITCHELL'S FOLD from an original 30, the tallest being nearly 7 ft. Rumours of a Shropshire trilithon were heard in the 18th century, but later dismissed by Aubrey Burl. The HOARSTONES (*shown below*) has 38 small stones with a central pillar.

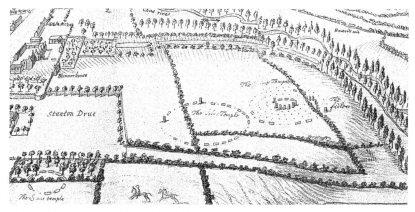

Above: Stanton Drew, as sketched by Stukeley in July 1723. To the west, not shown, is a three-stone Cove, similar to that at Avebury, now in the garden of The Druids Arms pub.

Above: The small, 97 ft north-easterly circle at Stanton Drew, near Bristol.

Above: The restored Devil's Quoit. The outer henge is c.492 ft (150m) wide, the stone circle is 225 ft (78m).

Above: The Kings Men at Rollright, built c. 2300 BC, with the King Stone shown in the field behind. The diameter of the Rollright stone circle is the same as that of the Sarsen Circle at Stonehenge.

Peak District & Isle of Man
north to the centre of the circle

Following the ancient trading route linking Avebury with Cumbria, we head north to the Peak District in Derbyshire.

Arbor Low, near Bakewell (*opposite*), consists of around 40 limestone menhirs, all fallen. Whether they originally stood upright is unknown. It had a henge and a stone cove, located in the centre of the circle (in contrast to its southern counterparts). Often called the 'Stonehenge of the North', Robin Heath places it within a landscape triangle connecting Stonehenge (*p. 17*) and Bryn Celli Ddu in Anglesey (*p. 37*).

Barbrook features three stone circles, the main one being a Type-B flattened circle (*see opposite, & page 13*). In patchy tree growth on Stanton Moor, a low stone circle called Nine Ladies (*below*) is located within a grand Bronze Age cemetery. To the southwest the Fiddlers Stone acts as an outlier, but has been moved several times. The Seven Stones of Hordron Edge occupy a delightful position overlooking the Derwent Valley. It had ten stones originally, but three are fallen. Earth lights and strange phenomena have been reported here.

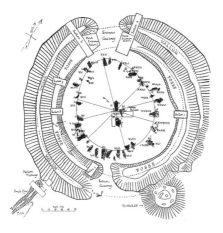

*Left, and above: Arbor Low, Derbyshire, with its
40-50 fallen stones, is an impressive egg-shaped
circle with a central cove, dated to around 2000
BC. An earthen avenue emerged from its south
side towards a huge barrow on Gib Hill.*

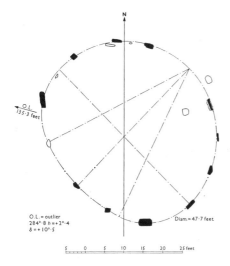

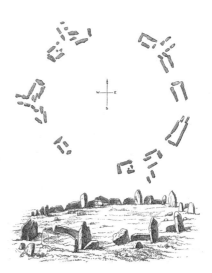

*Above left: Barbrook One (A. Thom); Barbrook Two is 300m north with 9 stones and a cairn.
Above right: The only stone circle on the ISLE OF MAN, MEAYLL (or Mull), near the folk village of Cregneish.
Probably a chambered tomb, with six grave-pairs arranged in a circle. Late Neolithic/early Bronze Age.
Opposite: Nine Ladies of Stanton Moor is within a Bronze Age cemetery (drawing by Steve Larder).*

YORKSHIRE & THE NORTH
high on the moors

High on the Yorkshire moors can be found hundreds of megaliths, some with remarkable rock art (*see opposite top left*). In the 19th century The TWELVE APOSTLES of Ilkley Moor (*opposite, centre*) was known as the *Druidical Dial*, as it was thought to be some kind of stone calendar. It once had 20 uprights with a central stone made of local millstone grit, but only 12 stones now remain, none taller than 4 ft. It forms a perfect isosceles triangle with two other circles, the GRUBSTONES and the BACKSTONES, both 1,300 megalithic yards away, and astronomical alignments have been suggested. Further north is a classic *four poster* (*see p. 39*) called the DRUID'S ALTAR near Skipton, sited in the same part of the moors as the APPLETREEWICK, DUMPIT HILL and GRASSINGTON circles.

In the sacred landscape of the Gypsey Race near Scarborough, the RUDSTON MONOLITH (*opposite*) is a staggering 25 ft, Britain's tallest. Also of note are the three spaced out DEVIL'S ARROWS (*below*). Between 18–22 ft tall they align with the nearby THORNBOROUGH HENGES.

The most northerly English stone ring is DUDDO FIVE STONES. Nearby is the huge ruined circle of HETHPOOL and its smaller sister.

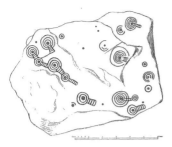 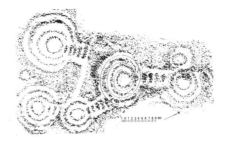

Above: Thom's analysis of the Panorama Stone on Ilkley Moor, near the Twelve Apostles stone circle.

Above: The Twelve Apostles. Balls of lights and UFOs are often reported at this site. After D. Starley.

Above: Rudston, with Britain's tallest menhir, 25 ft; Left: Cloughton Moor stone circle, East Yorkshire, with its holed stone; Facing page: The Devil's Arrows of Boroughbridge, North Yorkshire.

THE LAKE DISTRICT
stone circles as landscape art

Perhaps Britain's most beautifully sited circle, CASTLERIGG is also one of the oldest. Built around 3200 BC, it sits in magnificent open space surrounded by mountains, lakes and an ancient trackway (*see opposite*). Comprising 35 modestly sized stones, it is large, like other Cumbrian rings (108 ft at its longest diameter). Three cairns were discovered within the circle in 1856, and a huge stone axe nine years later.

LONG MEG AND HER DAUGHTERS (*below and opposite*) is the third largest stone circle in Britain. Meg herself, a 12 ft red sandstone outlier, with carved cups, rings, grooves, spirals and concentric circles, sits to the SW on a midwinter sunset alignment. LITTLE MEG, a tiny circle famous for its double-spiral carvings built about 1000 years later, sits to the NE.

SUNKENKIRK at Swinside was a favourite ceremonial centre for pagans in the 1970s and '80s. The grey stones are porphyritic slate, but its function is unclear; no astronomical alignments have been deduced.

Other sites: GREYCROFT, rebuilt in 1949, overlooks the Irish Sea and has 10 of its original basalt stones. BLAKELEY RAISE, a small stone circle, is on the far west of the Cumbrian Mountains, with 12 stones remaining, all under 3 feet. THE DRUIDS CIRCLE of Ulverston and BIRKRIGG (a rare concentric ring, featuring 20 outer and 12 inner stones) lie on the south Cumbrian coast. GAMELANDS CIRCLE is a larger affair, originally of 42 stones, and can be found at the foot of Knott Hill, east of the M6.

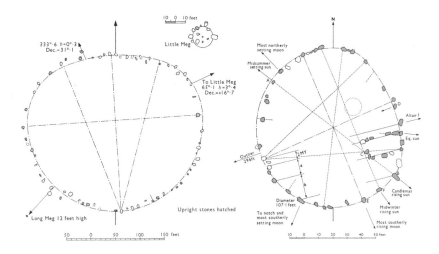

Above left and facing page: Long Meg and Her Daughters (A. Thom). The 69 granite 'daughters' are arranged in a 359 ft wide Type-B flattened circle (see page 137). Above right and below: Castlerigg stone circle, Keswick, a 108 ft wide Type-A flattened circle with strong astronomical alignments.

WALES & ANGLESEY
refuge of the Druids

Wales once had a thriving megalithic culture, and the stones still carry hundreds of legends of giants and associations with King Arthur.

CERRIG DUON ('Black Rock') is one of many rings in South Wales. The ovoid shape is about 70 ft in diameter, with an avenue heading northeast. Its mighty Maen Mawr stone weighs about ten tons and sits north of the circle; visible from a great distance, it still serves as a marker for travellers coming up from the Tawe Valley.

Heading northwest, high up in the Preseli Mountains, BEDD ARTHUR (Arthur's Grave) is an oval arrangement of small stones, overlooking the rocky outcrop of Carn Meini. The idea of the oval Bluestone 'horseshoe' at Stonehenge may have originated here. East of Aberystwyth, at YSBYTY CYNFYN near the famous Devil's Bridge, a Christianised stone circle is now part of the church wall. The tallest stone is 11 ft, and surviving menhirs mark the boundary of what could have been the largest megalithic site in Wales.

The DRUID'S CIRCLE, south of Penmaenmawr in North Wales, sits high on a wind-blown stretch of moorland. It was described by Edward Llwyd in 1695 as "the most remarkable monument in all Snowden". The extraordinary MOEL TY UCHAF (*see p. 402*), 'Hill of the Highest House', 1,375 ft above Merioneth, is, according to Keith Critchlow, "perhaps the most geometrically sophisticated of all Neolithic structures".

Anglesey is remembered as the last stronghold of the Druids. Its most famous surviving circle site—BRYN CELLI DDU—dates to 4800 BC and is now a chambered tomb oriented to the summer solstice sunrise, but once had an oval megalithic ring with about 17 stones (*shown on p. 180*).

Above: Druid's Circle in North Wales. An oval arrangement of some 30 granite stones.

Above: Bryn Celli Ddu, Anglesey, in 1847 and 150 years later, after restoration.

Above: Henblas Dolmen, Anglesey. These stones are latticed with thick veins of quartz.

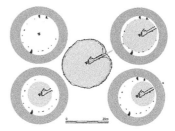

Above: Phases of Bryn Celli Ddu, anticlockwise from top left, showing stone circle.

Above: "The great Temple & Grove of the Druids at Trerdrew in Anglesea," known today as the Bryn Gwyn complex, recorded by Stukeley in his Itinerarium Curiousum *in 1725.*

LOWLAND SCOTLAND
and the borders

Southwest Scotland boasts many circles in a variety of styles (the southeast has only one of note—BORROWSTON RIG, *shown opposite*).

The oval shaped TWELVE APOSTLES near Dumfries is the largest in Scotland and the seventh largest in Britain. Mostly now destroyed, it was once nearly 300 ft across. GLENQUICKEN is a circular ring of 29 stones with a chunky granite pillar at its centre. Described by Aubrey Burl as 'the most perfect centre-stone circle in the British Isles,' it was here that a 'man of uncommon size' was unearthed in the 1800s.

TORHOUSEKIE is just as delightful, sitting on a raised terrace with 19 graded granite stones. It has been compared to Aberdeenshire's recumbent circles, although it probably dates from an earlier period.

Around Kilmartin, the small TEMPLEWOOD arrangement looks like a circle of gravestones; rightly so, as it is an ancient burial site (*see opposite*).

Loch Tay in Perthshire is surrounded by megalithic circles including CROFT MORAIG (*shown below, after Piggott & Simpson*), the ACHARN FALLS, KINNELL OF KILLIN, LEYS OF MARLEE, and FORTINGALL. Fortingall is a sunken triple circle with some cup marked stones, overlooked by Mount Schiehallion, or *Sidh Chailleann*, which translates as 'Fairy Hill'.

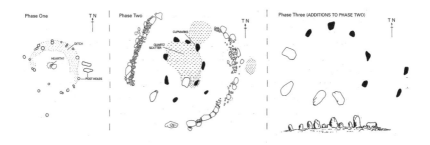

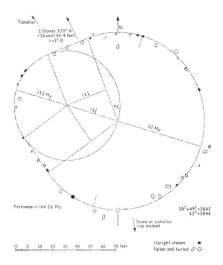

Tumulus

2 Stones 333°·4
126 and 135·4 feet
h =2°·0

15½ My

12½

15½

9½

25 My

Perimeter = 164·26 My

$38^2 + 49^2 = 3845$
$62^2 = 3844$

Stone at tumulus
cup marked

10 0   10 20 30 40 50 60   70 feet

Upright stones   ●
Fallen and buried ∅ ○

Left: Geometrical analysis of Borrowston Rig (A. Thom). Above: Lundin Links *in Fife. Once four stones, it is typical of a megalithic 'Four Poster' style found all over Scotland. Below: Templewood stone circle, in the extraordinary Kilmartin valley. It began life as a circle of twenty stones of local schist, and is dated to 3500 BC.*

Scottish Highlands
tracking the southernmost moon

Crossing into the Scottish Highlands reveals a few small circles, such as the one at KILLIN, Perthshire (*shown below right*). Further north, there are over 150 recumbent stone circles in Aberdeenshire (there were once many more). Built high up with a clear southern horizon, many of them feature a massive recumbent block, often up to 60 tons, oriented to the southwest (*e.g. below left, at DYCE*). Two upright 'flankers' sit either side creating a horizontal 'altar' or *false horizon*, which frames the path of the low midsummer, southernmost setting moon (*see opposite*). Some circles don't fit this astronomical scheme, and echo earlier examples dating to between 2700–2000BC. Many are burial sites with a cairn in the ring. MIDMAR KIRK is now in a churchyard.

Nearly 200 geometric carved stone spheres have been found in the Grampian area in the vicinity of stone circles. Tetrahedra, cubes, octahedra and icosahedra all fit into one's palm. Some, like the famous TOWIE BALL (*inset top left*), have beautiful spiral patterns.

Around Inverness, construction style changes. Several stone circles and ring cairns cluster at the head of Loch Ness. CLAVA CAIRNS are three burial sites with a SW orientation, all surrounded by 12 stones. CORRIMONY, to the southwest, is similar but larger. The simple DRUID TEMPLE is a perfect 'egg shaped ring' (*opposite top right*). Further north, rings get smaller, until we come to the giants in the islands.

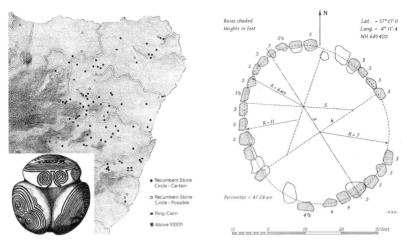

Above: Aubrey Burl's map of recumbent circles in Aberdeenshire; originally there were over 300.

Above: 3-4-5 Pythagorean triangles in the inner ring of the Druid Temple in Inverness (A. Thom).

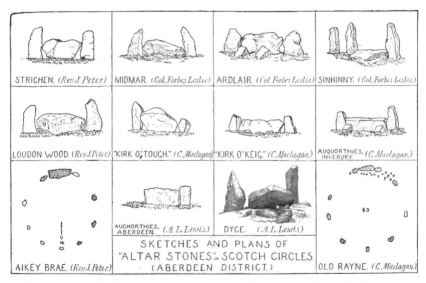

Above: A selection of Aberdeenshire's recumbent stone circles showing their 'altars' which frame the midsummer moonset, particularly its southernmost setting which occurs every 18.6 years.

THE SCOTTISH ISLANDS
the high art perfected

Most of the Scottish islands have stone circles. Some are small, lost, or hidden, others magnificent in their scale and beauty. On Arran, Auchagallon Cairn and Lamlash are two modest examples (15 and 7 stones respectively). Machrie Moor (*below left*) has several rings.

On Mull, two 8 ft menhirs remain of the Balliscate stone circle. On the south coast the 9 large stones of Lochbuie stand in the 'Field of the Druids'. In the south of Skye, Na Clachan Bhreige (false stones) sits amid beautiful scenery with three tall standing stones, and one fallen.

In the Outer Hebrides, the cruciform site of Callanish (*opposite top*) dominates the Isle of Lewis, its four avenues meeting at a circle of 12 impressive blades forming a Type-A flattened circle and enclosing a 15 ft central menhir. The nearby concentric circle of Cnoc Fillibhear Bheag and the smaller Gharraidh are also worth a visit. (*See too pp. 277-319.*)

The Orkney circles share Callanish's mystical quality, attracting hardened megalithomaniacs. The Ring of Brodgar (*opposite centre, and in the background of 2800 BC Maes Howe, below right*) is the largest in Scotland. Once known as *The Temple of the Sun*, its smaller companion, the Stones of Stenness (*opposite bottom*), was called *The Temple of the Moon*.

Callanish, on the Isle of Lewis, has the form of a Celtic cross (a circle with four avenues).

The Ring of Brodgar; 341 ft (104m) wide, 2500BC. A nearby site, the Ness of Brodgar, dates to 3300BC.

The Stones of Stenness; the henge was cut 2m into solid rock, removing 18,000 cubic metres of stone.

IRISH CIRCLES
justified and ancient

The oldest stone circles in the British Isles are found in Sligo, NW Ireland. The area around Knocknarea mountain has 1,450 megalithic tombs and 22 low lying 'Boulder Circles', like the one at the CARROWMORE complex (*opposite, top right*). Here, Swedish archaeologists have pushed construction back as far as 7490 BC, the oldest in Europe, long before the more famous sites appear in the Boyne Valley.

The mighty passage grave of NEWGRANGE in Co. Meath (*opposite bottom*) was once surrounded by a circle of stones which may have predated the main structure; some still remain. Nearby, KNOWTH and DOWTH (also passage graves) are each propped up by circles of beautifully carved stones.

South of Dublin in Co. Wicklow are the ATHGREANY PIPER STONES with a midsummer sunrise alignment and one unusually large cup-mark. BROADLEAS, 105 ft across, is oval, like many in Cumbria.

Southern Ireland has many stone rings of different sizes and shapes. DROMBEG in Cork is one of 80 that resemble the Aberdeenshire recumbents, only smaller. Many Limerick circles, like the tiny LISSYVIGGEEN in Co. Kerry or the enormous LIOS CIRCLE near Bruff, are set within an earthen bank. KEALKIL is utterly charming.

In Co. Donegal, Northern Ireland, the beautifully set BELTANY RING dates from the end of the British circle-building era around 1400 BC. Cup-marked, it was once a tomb, and aligns to the May Day sunrise. In Ulster, there are several low rings of small stones built after 1900 BC. These are multiple sites with cairns in their centres, or nearby, some have avenues, such as BEAGHMORE STONE CIRCLES in Co. Tyrone.

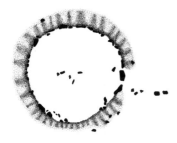

Above: Castleruddery, County Wicklow, with outer bank and eastern entrance.

Above: Circle 7, Carrowmore, with central small dolmen, & Knocknarea Mountain with cairns (Brennan, 1982).

Above: Greidle, Co. Down, N. Ireland. Six stones of a court remain, two leading to a gallery.

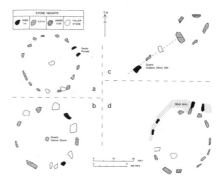

Above: Four stone circles from Cork. a: Carrigagulla SW; b. Currebeha; c. Knockraheen; d. Carrigagrenane (from Burl, after Barber, 1972).

Above: Entrance stone at Newgrange.
Below: Newgrange before excavation.

GERMANY & SCANDINAVIA
burials for the dead

Scandinavia is famous for its majestic stone ships. Shaped like longboats, many of these circle-type constructions are grave sites. However, the iconic ALE'S STONES (*below*) in Skåne, Sweden, shows no trace of burial. It aligns to winter solstice sunrise and summer solstice sunset. A stone ship was added in the 10th century to an existing Bronze Age mound at SKIBSSAETNING. It is common in this part of the world for sites to date from the Neolithic up to the Viking era, as megalith builders suffered less from Christians vandalising and re-dedicating their sites.

There are twelve known circles in Norway, the most important being HUNN GRAVFELT on the Østfold 'Prehistoric Road'. At this site are nine stone circles and a number of burial mounds dating to about 1200 BC. On one of the stones is a runic carving. LUNDEBY TINGSTED is another fine example consisting of three small circles.

Poland has some fantastic sites. Officially dated to around 300 AD the ODRY RING COMPLEX in Pomorskie (*opposite, centre*) is now thought to have been built around 2000 BC. Twelve stone circles range from 15m to 33m in diameter and comprise between 16 and 29 stones.

Germany is more known for its chambered dolmens, but in the North some stone circles (Ger. *steinkreis*) lie hidden in the woods. BOITIN STEINTANZ (*steintanz* = 'stone dance') in Western Pomerania is a group of four stone circles. Nearby NETZEBAND is another example.

Above: 1880s reconstruction of ancient burial site, ROESKILDE, Denmark, typical to the area.

Below: Odry, Poland, has many burial mounds and twelve 15-33m stone circles, each of 16 to 29 stones, 20-70cm high, many with central menhirs. Three rings point to winter solstice sunrise, another three to summer solstice sunrise.

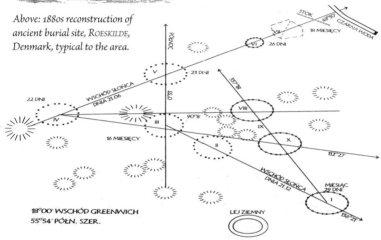

Facing page: Swedish stone boats at WISKEHÄRAD, Halland, and Ale's Stones, c.500 AD, C Hilfeling, 1777.

Left: 1880s watercolour by Olof Hermelin of the GREBY PREHISTORIC GRAVE FIELDS, Sweden, with battlefield burial mounds, stone circles and single monoliths.

FRANCE, SPAIN & PORTUGAL
all shapes and sizes

Some of the oldest and largest megaliths in the world are at CARNAC, Brittany (*opposite centre*). A vast complex, of global significance, its approximately 45 circles (French *cromlechs,* from the Welsh *crwmllech*) can be egg-shaped, horse-shoes, or rectangular or square.

Although French cromlechs often differ from their British counterparts, in the early 19th century an English-style oval on the ISLET OF BENIGUET in Finistere was illustrated showing 12 stones in the Cornish style (*see opposite*). Also off the north coast, in a tidal zone on the ISLE OF CHAUCEY, is a curious circle of 40 stones, completely submerged at high tide. In the south, LACAM DE PEYRARINES in Languedoc is a very British affair: a huge oval 340 by 290 feet wide with a central menhir. Nearby, LACAM DE LA RIGALDERIE is slightly smaller with 36 stones.

The border area between France and Spain has many small cromlechs, often clustered together, with some dating from well into the Iron Age. Hundreds are dotted across the Pyrenees. On the western extreme a notable 'four poster' called MENDILUZE HARRESPILA in Pais Vasco is officially dated to around 800 BC.

Portugal has some spectacular sites (*below, and see caption opposite*).

Above: Early 19th century drawing of a stone circle on ILE BENIGUET, *Finistere, France, now destroyed.*

Top right: Dolmen at Crucuno, Carnac. Above: Menec West Cromlech, Carnac. Dated to 4500 BC, it is perhaps the earliest prototype, egg-shaped ring. It is attached to multiple stone rows.

Almendres I
(Neolítico antigo-médio)

Almendres II
(Neolítico médio)

Almendres III
(Neolítico final)

Above and right: Portugal has some of the finest and oldest cromlechs in Europe. Near Evora is the 8,000-year-old CROMELEQUE DOS ALMENDRES *with rounded granite stones, and nearby dolmens. From this 92-stone circle the midwinter sun rises above the 8ft* MENHIR DO ALMENDRES, *1km to the southeast. Two similar cromlechs called* PORTELA DE MOGOS *and* VALE DO MEIO *are located nearby; as is the square* XEREZ *(opposite), dated to 4000 BC.*

MALTA & NORTH AFRICA
and the Senegambian circles

Malta is home to many temples: MNAJDRA and HAGAR QIM (*see p. vi*), and the Xaghra complex on the isle of Gozo (*see opposite*). Further south, in Morocco, the MSOURA ring can be found near Asilah. This is a huge ellipse, 195 ft (59.29m) by 185 ft (56.18m); 168 stones survive out of the original 175. A later, part-excavated tumulus sits in its centre.

Near Cyrenaica in Libya a stone circle was recorded in 1882, and other trilithons and dolmens litter the north African coast. Hundreds of prehistoric tumuli, stelae and megalithic structures are located about 60 miles west of Abu Simbel in southern Egypt. A small egg-shaped stone ring called NABTA PLAYA (*see below*) was found in 1974 in the Nubian Desert; at 7,000 years old, it is the oldest so far discovered in Africa.

There are 93 stone circles in Senegal and Gambia, dated 300 BC–1600 AD, and divided between SINE NGAYENE and WANAR in Senegal, and WASSU and KERBATCH in Gambia (*below right*). The laterite stones are cylindrical or polygonal with the heaviest weighing around 7 tons.

In the Mpumalanga region of South Africa, a striking and ancient 100 ft stone circle called ADAM'S CALENDAR was discovered in 2003.

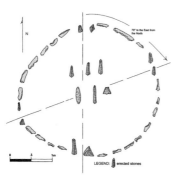

LEGEND: erected stones

Left: Nabta Playa is a Type 1 egg-shaped circle, dated to 5000 BC, aligned to the summer solstice sunrise. Below: Circles at Kerbatch, Gambia.

Above: Msoura, in northern Morocco, is a stone ellipse constructed using a 12-35-37 Pythagorean triangle (similar to over 30 British examples).

Above: 19th century photograph of megalithic trilithons in Libya, resembling those of Stonehenge. Another one can be found at ELKEB, near Tripoli.

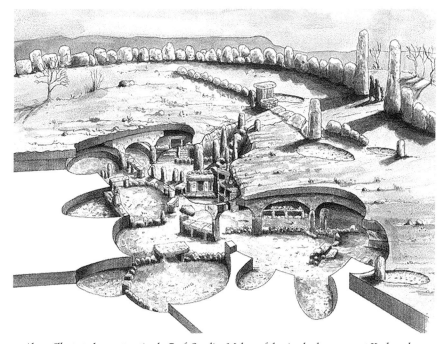

Above: Illustrated reconstruction by Prof. Caroline Malone of the circular hypogeum at Xaghra, close to the nearby larger site of Ggantija on the Maltese island of Gozo. The site dates from 4100-2500 BC. Around a quarter of a million bones and objects from 800 individuals were discovered in underground chambers below the stone circle during excavations in the 1980s. The site is now closed to the public.

THE AMERICAS
circles north and south

In North America, hundreds of stone chambers, dolmens and menhirs stretch across New England and New York state. Within this hidden megalithic landscape are two stone circles, BURNT HILL (*opposite, top left*) and THE DRUIDS CIRCLE. In 1602, Spanish explorer Sebastian Vizcaino visited Catalina Island, California, with chronicler Father Torquemada and described a ceremonial complex "formed by a large circle of long stones pointing upward toward the mid-day sun".

The 'Stonehenge of the Amazon', CALÇOENE MEGALITHIC OBSERVATORY, is located on a hilltop near Calçoene, Amapa, Brazil. Here, 127 blocks of granite, up to 11 ft tall, are spaced at regular intervals around the hill, like a crown. The 100ft circle is thought to have been constructed by the Amapán people between the 1st and 10th century AD. It has a winter solstice sunrise alignment.

SILLUSTANI, near Lake Titicaca in Peru, is well known for its huge hilltop funerary towers called 'Chulpas' (*opposite top right*). On the plains below are several astronomically-aligned stone circles built by the Kolla (a pre-Inca culture) between 100 AD and 1600 AD. The largest, at 34 ft, is INTIWATANA (*shown opposite*), which translates as "to moor the sun".

Above: Burnt Hill, Heath, Massachusetts. Inspiration for H.P. Lovecraft's Sentinel Hill in The Dunwhich Horror: 'Oldest of all are the great rings of rough-hewn stone columns on the hilltops, but these are more generally attributed to the Indians than to the settlers'.

Opposite Page: Calçoene, Brazil.   Above: Intiwatana, Peru, in 1877, one of six stone circles at Sillustani.   Above, top right: The plateau is dominated by Chulpas—megalithic round towers.

Karahunge & Middle East
lost circles of the Bible

Armenia boasts one of the oldest, most impressive circles in the world. Called Zorats Karer or Karenish by the locals, and widely known as Armenia's Stonehenge, Karahunge has 223 standing stones that vary between 2ft and 9ft tall and weigh up to 10 tons (*see opposite*). 80 stones have circular holes drilled through them, 37 are still standing.

There are 39 mentions in the Bible of Gilgal, a 'circle of standing stones'. In one account, after miraculously crossing the river Jordan, Joshua orders the Israelites to take twelve large stones from the river bed, one for each tribe, and place them at Gilgal 'in memory'. Gilgal has been identified with the village of Jiljilia, about 8m north of Bethel.

In present-day Israel, the submerged site of Atlit Yam (*opposite bottom*) near Haifa dates from 6900–6300 BC and is the earliest known evidence for an agro-pastoral-marine subsistence system on the Levantine coast. A stone semicircle containing seven half-ton monoliths was discovered at a depth of 8–12m. The stones have cup marks carved into them, and surround a freshwater spring.

Above: Karahunge (speaking stones). 17 of the stones align to sunrise and sunset at the solstices and equinoxes, and 14 to lunar extremes. Russian prehistorian Professor Paris Herouni analysed a prominent holed stone and found that it aligned to Deneb, the brightest star of Cygnus, c.5500 BC.

Opposite page: Two illustrations of the stone circle complex in DARABGIRD, Iran. The lozenge-shaped stones are similar to those at Avebury and other sites in Britain.

Left: Reconstruction of the submerged stone circle at Atlit Yam, Haifa, Israel.

FAR EAST & DOWN UNDER
from India to Australia

Northern Pakistan is home to several stone circles. Local legend has it that the 30-stone Asota ring at Kalula (*opposite top*) was erected by *Ashoka* (Buddha) so he could meditate at one each day of the month.

India has a rich megalithic heritage, including around 300 prehistoric low stone circles in Junapani, Maharashtra state, dated to 1000 BC. In the Dekkan region, stone circles were still being built in the 1800s (*see example below*), while the massive Mudumal Stone Circle in Telangana (*opposite, centre right*) is now thought to date to 5000 BC.

In Northern Japan, about 30 stone rings were built by the Jomon culture between 2400 BC and 1000 BC, a fine example can be seen at Oshoro, where there is a 22 by 33m oval, with an internal circle.

In Australia, at Wurdi Youang, Victoria, a 165 ft circle, possibly 11,000 years old, of over 100 basalt boulders aligns to the sunsets on the solstices and equinoxes. At Mullumbimby, in New South Wales, two extremely ancient circles were once linked by an avenue (*see opposite*).

Asota (Kalula) stone circle in Northern Pakistan—one of many in this area.

Above left: Dolmen and circles at PULLICONDAH, near Madras, India.   Above right: Mudumal Stone Circle in Telangana, India, is 7,000 years old and has a cup-mark carving of the Big Dipper.

Above: Mullumbimby, New South Wales, Australia. 181 standing stones, on a 100m long boomerang-shaped mound, once formed two circles linked by an avenue, overlooking Byron Bay. The site is now thought to be extremely ancient. A large, partly excavated tumulus is located less than 100 yards away.

MODERN STONE CIRCLES
the renaissance of megalithomania

Few stone circles were constructed in Europe after 1000 BC. However, in Indonesia and other remote nations, some tribes still get together and quarry, transport and build megalithic structures.

The first modern circle in Britain was probably inspired by John Aubrey. On midsummer's day in 1717 the Irish author J. J. Toland held a meeting for Druids in London on PRIMROSE HILL, London (*see opposite*), and established *The Ancient Druid Order*. Later in the 18th century, this inspired Iolo Morganwg [1747-1826] to form the *Gorsedd of the Bards of the Isle of Britain*. Some years later again, around 1800, a ring of stones was constructed around the great Pontypridd "rocking stone" in Wales, due to its popularity as a pagan ritual site (*see opposite*).

Since the 1960s, individuals, festivals (*e.g. opposite top right*) and organisations the world over have built an estimated 200 stone circles. There is even one in the middle of a roundabout in MILTON KEYNES, UK. Other notable examples include: HAM HILL in Somerset, HILLY FIELDS in Lewisham, London, and MARYHILL war memorial in Washington, US, a concrete replica of Stonehenge which has nevertheless been found to have interesting acoustic properties. Megalith builders such as Rob Roy and Ivan McBeth have constructed numerous rings using ancient techniques from England to New England.

The prehistoric sites detailed in this book may represent a golden age of astronomy, earth mysteries and technological prowess. However, with a new wave of megalithomania sweeping the planet, more will surely be built, leaving future archaeologists and antiquarians just as baffled as we are now! The power of the ancients has come full circle.

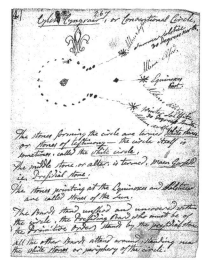

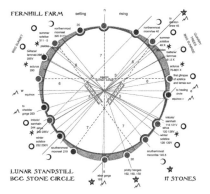

Above: Design for a stone circle for the 2006 Big Green Gathering by J. Martineau & S. Kirwan.

Left: Plan for a stone circle from the famous Druid revival meeting on Primrose Hill in 1792.

PONTYPRIDD ROCKING STONE, Glamorgan. In 1795, a gorsedd meeting took place around the huge slab of natural slate stone (the Maen Chwyf). The circle was a later addition. In 1899 a formal plan for future stone circles was produced. Until recently, one was constructed at each annual Eisteddfod so there are now numerous modern stone circle across Wales (and even Hungary and Patagonia).

(Vue prise dans le champ de Carnac, département du Morbihan.)

CARNAC

Howard Crowhurst

Above: Druidical gathering and blessing around a sacred menhir, Paris, 1880.

INTRODUCTION

Carnac. Most people have heard of it, and see in their mind's eye lines of standing stones crossing the landscape. Few realise the depth of the enigma and the problem it poses to our model of history.

These megalithic monuments are far older than the ones found in the British Isles. Some of them are also much bigger. Recent research has dated the foundations of a giant standing stone to 6200 BC which is in the Mesolithic period, or intermediate stone age.

Another astonishing fact is the sheer number of them. The Carnac alignments, the best preserved of the stone avenues, contain today slightly over 3000 stones. In 1892, the antiquarian Félix Gaillard counted 1000 stones standing and 5000 recumbent in the rows at nearby Erdeven, despite many years of daily use as a quarry.

There is no written or oral mention of the people who built them, although stories persist of an ancient race of giants. The Celts must have noticed the stones c.1000 BC when they first arrived in the area but there is no account of them meeting (or fighting) a pre-existing civilisation. When Roman war ships arrived in Armorica (the old name for Brittany) in around 60 BC, they initially met ferocious opposition from the local Venetes who had better boats (according to Caesar). Indeed, many Roman remains have been found in megalithic sites, including coins which they left among the stones for luck.

When the Romans pulled out, pagan places of worship were a target for fervent Catholics, encouraged by Charlemagne and various popes. Then, after the French revolution, megaliths silently suffered destruction by stone quarriers and farmers for financial gain.

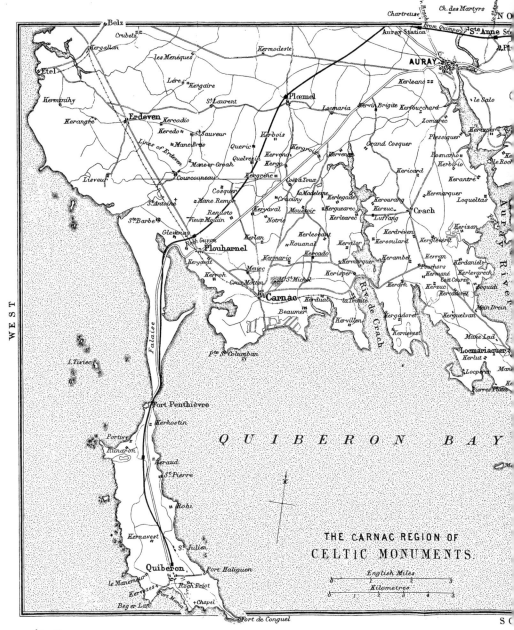

THE CARNAC REGION OF
CELTIC MONUMENTS.

English Miles

Kilometres

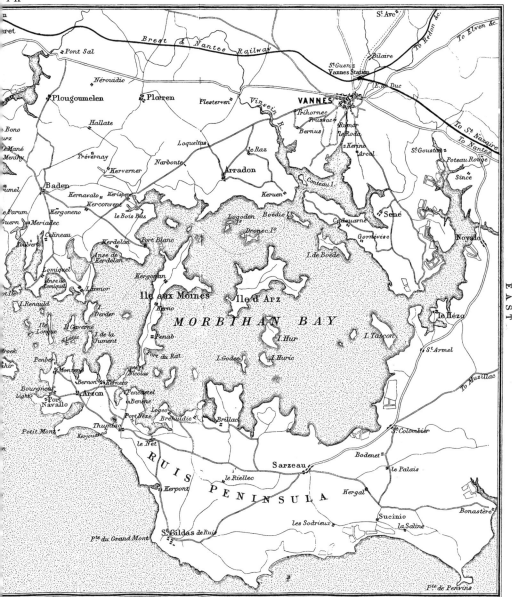

THE BAY OF QUIBERON
rich in history

The South Morbihan coast in Brittany has been inhabited for about 500,000 years. After the last ice age, during the Mesolithic period (10,000–6000 BC) a population of fishermen-hunter-gatherers settled there and buried their dead in low earth mounds. A necropolis found on the island of Téviec off the west coast of Quiberon, containing about 30 skeletons, showed elaborate burial rituals.

Today, the area is densely populated, despite the land being the most expensive in Brittany; building continues, destroying visibility and the special atmosphere still to be found in more remote sites.

Archaeologists have estimated that between 85% and 90% of the megaliths in the area have disappeared. But despite this, 900,000 people come to visit each year and feel the magic that still oozes off the ancient stones.

Facing page: La Table des Marchands dolmen at Locmariaquer. Above: According to ancient folk tales, it was a lost race of giants who built the megaliths. Below: The Kermario alignments with ships harboured in the Quiberon Bay when a sea view still existed (1835).

Pl. 4.

A High Density Monument
the little that's left

Although much has now gone, the Bay of Quiberon region still has the highest concentration of major megalithic monuments in the world. In an area going from the eastern side of the Morbihan Gulf to the Quiberon peninsula, a distance of about 20km, and spreading inland from the coast for around 10km are to be found:

Six large stone alignments and several remains of smaller ones, seven massive tumuli; at least ten cromlechs or stone circles; two quadrilateral enclosures; over 200 dolmens, five of which contain many engravings and many that still have their cairn around them;

and countless isolated menhirs (or standing stones) the largest being Le Grand Menhir Brisé at Locmariaquer, now recumbent but once nearly 20m high. Others, still standing at Kerzerho, are 6.5m tall.

Recent research has also shown the presence of megaliths on the sea floor in the Bay of Quiberon and even on the islands out to sea. Remains of the alignments at Saint Pierre Quiberon can be found on the beach at very low tides but they extend into the sea for over a kilometre. The sea level was between 5 and 7 metres lower than today and this corresponds to the average depth of the bay which could consequently have been a vast plain crossed by several rivers. Whether it was flooded progressively or by a sudden rise in sea level is not clear.

AN ANCIENT ARCHITECTURE
and the first pictures of Carnac

The Carnac area displays a variety of different kinds of monuments.

The *Menhir* (from two Breton words *men* = stone and *hir* = long), can be found standing alone, or in single or multiple alignments, or in curves (*cromlech*) or rectangles (*quadrilaterals*), or lying *recumbent*.

The *Dolmen* (*dol* = table) is a chamber and/or corridor where massive horizontal stones are placed on upright support stones. In some of the larger dolmens, the enormous cover stones are made from a stone called orthogneiss, a layered stone which is well-suited to being placed horizontally. Most of the dolmens were initially covered over by a *cairn* (a mound built with small stones).

The *Tumulus* is an artificial hill, much bigger than a cairn. Mud and clay were applied in layers to make it waterproof. The inner chambers often have no corridors and are enclosed in the centre of the mound. Many of these monuments were unknown until the middle of the 19th century as they were thought to be natural.

The first mention of these strange monuments is by Christophe-Paul de Robien, president of the Brittany Parliament, in 1725.

Opposite: Erdeven alignments. Above and below: Carnac alignments. All from Monumens Celtiques, *by Jacques de Cambry [1749-1807]. These exaggerated engravings of megaliths led to disappointment by visitors and sarcastic remarks by Flaubert. De Cambry founded "Celtomania," a mixture of neo-druidism and passion for the megaliths, which dominated in France for 70 years.*

BLAIR & RONALDS
the scientific method

Many early etchings of the Carnac alignments show 20 or more rows of perfectly aligned stones, all at least 10 metres high. So when two British explorers, Alexander Blair and Sir Francis Ronalds, came to visit in 1832, they were rather disappointed by what they found, and became convinced that they hadn't yet discovered the real alignments. When the truth began to dawn on them, however, they immediately began to remedy the situation and correct the exaggerated reports by compiling a good number of very precise drawings. These remain extremely valuable to archaeologists today during attempts to reconstruct the initial layout of the megaliths.

Blair and Ronalds' effort to create a more accurate view of the Carnac megaliths was continued by two more British antiquarians, William Collins Lukis and Sir Henry Dryden, who spent the two summer months in the area from 1871 to 1876, making detailed plans and precise watercolours. Unfortunately, much of their good work was destroyed by a fire at the printers. Luckily for us, however, during their visit they had initiated a Frenchman to their methods who would have a huge impact on the site: Felix Gaillard.

Above: A realistic representation of the Carnac alignments, complete with grazing wild horses and flock of birds, c.1890.

Left: Ronalds & Blair demonstrate the scientific method. From 1871-1876 they measured the exact height of many of the larger stones of Carnac.

Facing page: The recumbent Table Stone at the start of the Le Menec alignments in Carnac. A typically accurate drawing by Ronalds & Blair. Many of their images are used throughout this book.

Nodier & Taylor

a picturesque and romantic journey

The three plates on this page are some of the finest images of Carnac ever produced. They are drawn from *Voyages Pittoresques et Romantiques dans l'Ancienne France*, a monumental work directed by Baron Isidore Taylor and published as 24 volumes containing 3282 lithographs between 1820 and 1878. It was the first catalogue of French heritage sites, once again aiming to restore a rational image to France's past.

The two volumes on Brittany written by Charles Nodier were published in 1845 and 1846.

Below: Eastern end of the Erdeven alignments, today surrounded by woodland.
Opposite: Upper: Kermario, head of the line, looking west. Lower: Le Menec middle, looking west.

FELIX GAILLARD
Alfred Devoir & Dr. Marcel Baudouin

The preservation of the megaliths in the Carnac area is greatly due to Felix Gaillard [1832-1910]. He fought to have the stones classified as historical monuments (bringing an end to their use as building material), published papers of his excavations and opened the world's first megalithic museum in Plouharnel. From 1892 onwards he published a series of papers in a French scientific review explaining how the monuments were orientated towards sunrises and sunsets at solstices and equinoxes. In his book *Astronomie Préhistorique*, he presented graphics showing the orientation of 223 dolmens from southern Brittany, showing that not one had its opening between west and northeast, deducing that dolmen corridors were not positioned accidentally and were linked to the sun.

This archaeo-astronomical interpretation was further developed by Sir Norman Lockyer, Alfred Devoir and Dr Marcel Baudouin.

ANTIQUITIES OF CARNAC, IN BRITTANY: THE LINES OF CARNAC, FROM KARNAC, LOOKING EAST.

Above: The Kermario alignments shown as if they were on a cliff by the sea (they are in fact 2.4 km from the coast), 1835, Buttura and Chamoin. Facing page: The start of the Le Menec alignments, showing, on the right side, the remains of the cromlech at Le Menec West.

Left and below: Many 19th century engravings fancifully depicted the megalithcs as rows of petrified roman soldiers, as was suggested in popular folk tales of the time.

THE ERDEVEN ALIGNMENTS
captured by Commander Fréminville

Although less well known, the Erdeven alignments were initially much bigger than those at Carnac. The tallest menhirs (up to 6.5m) and the biggest stones (77 tonnes) in the area are to be found there.

Towards the end of the 19th century, after many years of destruction for building purposes, Félix Gaillard counted 1000 stones still standing and 5000 lying on the ground. He estimated that there may have been up to 50 rows of stones initially. For many years this was seen as highly exaggerated, until a study by Nantes University in 2003 on the stone rows at Saint-Pierre Quiberon (13 km to the south) showed that there must once have been 20 lines there, twice as many as in Carnac.

The Erdeven alignments can still be walked for around 4 km.

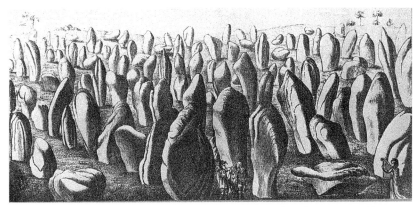

Left : A detail of the central part of the Erdeven alignments, seen from the Mane Bras dolmens. Above and below: Two engravings by Chevalier de Fréminville [1787-1848] of the Erdeven alignments, with the lines runing along a slope. Much destruction has taken place since.

The Erdeven lines are orientated along an east-west axis. They begin 6.27 km exactly north-west of the beginning of the Le Menec rows, at the start the Carnac alignments. Observation of sunrise and sunset can be made along the lines at equinoxes. There is free access all year round.

DOLMENS EVERYWHERE
giants' houses

Over 200 dolmens can be found in the area around Carnac. Some of these contain engravings which can still be seen today: Gavrinis, Mane Kerioned (Carnac), Le Petit Mont (Arzon), L'île Longue (not accessible to the public), La Table des Marchands, Mané Lud, Mané Ruthual and Les Pierres Plates (Locmariaquer), Le Tumulus de Kercado (Carnac). Some recently re-erected standing stones also have perfectly preserved carvings on the sides which laid on the ground: Menhir du Bronzo (Locmariaquer), Kermaillard (Arzon).

In Gavrinis (*see pages 84-85, & 378-382*), there is an engraving of a bovine with immense semi-circular horns on the upper (hidden) side of the cover stone. The animal's feet seemed to continue on the visible (inner) side of the huge cover stone of La Table des Marchands dolmen at Locmariaquer (*below, 3860m due west of Gavrinis*), suggesting that earlier monuments had been broken up and integrated into later constructions.

Above (overgrown, c.1840) and below (cleared, 1868): La Roche aux Fées at Essé (35 km SE of Rennes). 42 stones of various sizes, 17 planted along the SW side and 15 along the NE, with 9 as the roof and 1 for the door. The midwinter sun shines down the alley to the end of the chamber.

How Did They Do It?

rolling down the river

Although this work went on for about 3000 years, from 6000 BC to 3000 BC with a renewed construction period around 2500 BC, it seems unlikely that it was carried out solely by locals (archaeological remains indicate a population density of approximately 0.8 inhabitants per square km). In addition, certain massive stones in orthogneiss, like Le Grand Menhir Brisé (*see page 86*) weighing over 300 tons, were not local and must have been transported over 10km. In 2010, the remains of an 80 ton orthogneiss standing stone were found on the island of Belle Ile, south of the tip of the Quiberon peninsula, which was not linked to the coast at that time. This stone must have been moved over more than 30km, at least partially by sea.

No explanation using ropes and logs as rollers or floaters can account for how these enormous blocks of granite were moved. This has led to all kinds of hypotheses: levitation, granite concrete manufacture and extra terrestrial intervention. The truth is we simply do not know.

Facing page : The Crucuno dolmen (Blair & Ronalds, 1832). Above: Dolmen of Mané Lud, Locmariaquer. Below: La Table des Marchands at Locmariaquer with engraved end stone.

GAVRINIS
a womb with a view

Along the island of Gavrinis in the Morbihan Gulf flows one of the strongest currents in Europe. Permanent whirlpools announce one of the best preserved and finest architectural masterpieces of the Carnac builders' culture. The cairn of Gavrinis, an urchin-shaped mound with an average diameter of about 30m, covers a dolmen built with 1 quartz and 29 granite upright stones, 27 of which are covered with engravings. A long (13.4m), very slightly winding corridor leads to a small chamber (2m x 3m and 1.8m high) comprising 8 menhirs and a massive cover stone, supported by the cairn and not by the uprights.

On sunrise at winter solstice, the Sun's first rays redden an engraving of semicircles on the last stone before the chamber on the left hand side of the corridor. Then, a laser-like beam runs along the floor of the chamber and hits the left side of the left of the two stones which form the back wall. As the Sun comes up, the beam slowly widens and sinks, illuminating the left stone before it hits the floor (*see too pp. 378–382*).

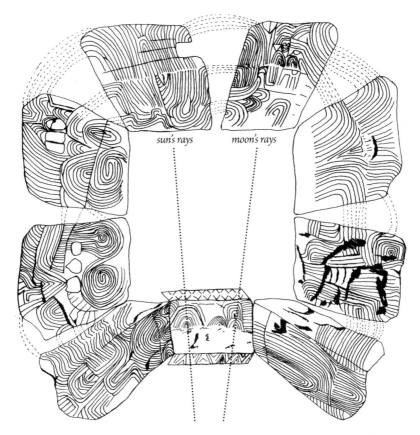

sun's rays   moon's rays

Above: The end chamber at Gavrinis (drawing AAK). The stone at the top right receives moonlight every 18.6 years when the Moon rises at its most southerly point (witnessed by the author in March 2007.) The engravings on these two stones link together at the centre, seemingly expressing a mystical marriage of the Sun and the Moon. Their hypothetical crossing point in the corridor is marked by a quartz stone (below). 'Gavrinis' may derive from Breton-Welsh roots; Gawr = giant or powerful man and Inis = island.

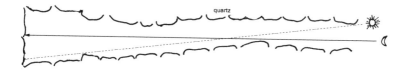

quartz

LE GRAND MENHIR BRISÉ
the stone at the centre of the world

At Locmariaquer lies the gigantic fallen and broken giant, *Le Grand Menhir Brisé*, called *Er Groah* (the fairy) in Breton. Thom suggested Le Grand Menhir was an important foresight for long distance lunar alignments (*opposite*). Made from Orthogneiss, this 20m long sculpted monster, weighing over 300 tons, now lies on the ground in four pieces, the base having fallen in one direction and the three upper parts in another. Serge Cassen suggested a powerful earthquake, 9.1 on the Richter scale, might have twisted the base. Orthogneiss is not local, so the stone it must have been transported over at least 12km, most probably from a quarry in Conleau at the Eastern end of the Morbihan Gulf. This extraction site is upstream along the Vannes River, so some people have suggested that it was floated downstream!

Orthogneiss is a layered stone, which makes lateral fracturing extremely difficult. However, Le Grand Menhir is broken *across* the grain in very smooth cuts, with no sign of chiselling.

Above and left: Le Grand Menhir in the 19th century. The bottom part, which has a plough/scale/ whale sculpted in bas relief, is perfectly aligned along the the axis of the Er Grah tumulus which heads N18.5°W from the base for about 160m while the three upper parts are to its east.

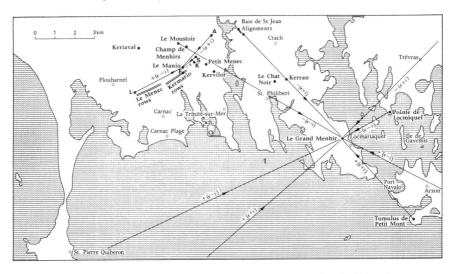

Above: Professor Alexander Thom saw the Grand Menhir as a central foresight for long distance lunar observations and indeed many monuments are placed on the major (ε+i) and minor (ε-i) extreme Moon positions (picture from John Edwin Wood, after Thom).

La Table des Marchands

sun and moon together soon

About 50m NE of the Grand Menhir lies La Table des Marchands dolmen, now covered by a debated cairn, reconstructed in 1991. The oldest images of the site show the orthogneiss cover stone, supported at three points by uprights, open to view, the surrounding mound being half the height of the monument. Inside the chamber, the ceiling is about 2.7m high. It has a complex engraving containing an axe-head plough, a Bishop's crook shape, a possible moon crescent and the feet of the animal at Gavrinis (*opposite, lower right*).

An upright ogival white stone with unique carvings, 'the Goddess', forms the end roof pillar (*opposite, lower left, and see too page 83*). Like Saint Louis' arch, the base and height are equal. Unfortunately, the engravings on the back of the stone are no longer visible.

The corridor has the same orientation as Gavrinis, so the winter solstice sunrise illuminates the left side of the Goddess while the major south moonrise lights its right side. The white stone, a kind of limestone, is rich in quartz and sparkles in even the faintest light.

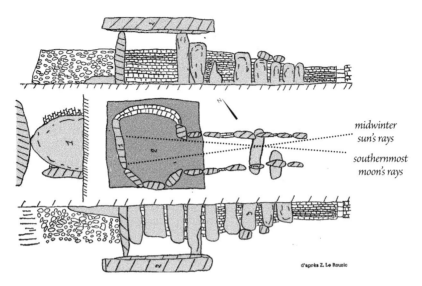

midwinter
sun's rays

southernmost
moon's rays

d'après Z. Le Rouzic

Above and Opposite page: La Table des Marchands. The axis of the corridor aligns on the Mane Er Hroëck tumulus and Le Petit Mont cairn to the SE and the Kerran dolmens to the NW (p.82).

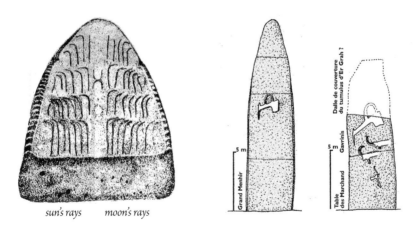

sun's rays   moon's rays

Dalle de couverture du tumulus d'Er Grah ?

Grand Menhir   5 m

5 m   Gavrinis

Table des Marchand

Left: The Goddess, end stone. Right: The cover stone, part of a once larger stone, a second part of which now forms one of the cover stones at Gavrinis (p.84-85), at the same latitude.

THE CRUCUNO RECTANGLE
looking at things from the right angle

Some 400m to the east of the hamlet of Crucuno in Plouharnel lies a rectangle, constructed on a man-made plateau, composed of 22 large menhirs, one of which is recumbent. It was restored in 1884 by Félix Gaillard who re-erected 14 of them, those for which he had found the wedging stones still in the ground. A plan made by Lukis and Dryden in 1874 shows the state of the site before any work was done. The line on the west side was virtually intact and it is orientated exactly to true north. This means that the rectangle as a whole is perfectly aligned to the cardinal directions.

The NE corner-SW corner diagonal has an angle of 36.87° to the south of east, which is the exact angle of a 3-4-5 triangle. This also happened to be the angle of sunrise at winter solstice 7000 years ago at this latitude. Today, it has moved north by about 0.8°, a little more than its own size on the horizon.

The vast megalithic ensemble in and around Carnac could not have been built solely by the local population. This could indicate that this latitude was chosen for its unique astro-geometrical qualities. It also shows the importance of the right angle.

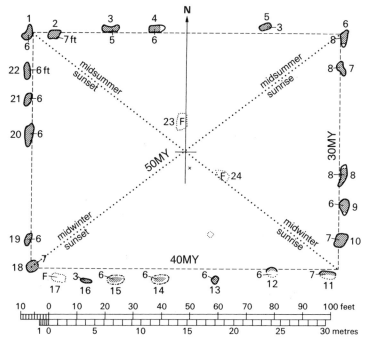

Above: *Thom's survey of the Crucuno rectangle, showing it is a clear 3:4 rectangle, aligned NSEW, with diagonals (length 5), that give the solstice sunrises and sunsets.*

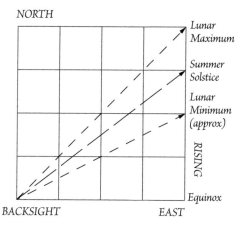

Left: *At the latitude of Carnac, the rising positions of the Sun and the Moon have an astonishing geometrical relationship. Over 18.6 years, the Moon's northerly rising moves north and south of the Sun's summer solstice position. When the Moon is furthest north (e.g. in 2006), it is at 45°, along the diagonal of a square from the observer's position. 9½ years later (e.g. in 2015) it is on the diagonal of a double square at its extreme northern position.*

CARNAC ASTROGEOMETRY
sun, moon and right angle

Aligned on the axis of Gavrinis is the 3m tall menhir at Kermaillard. In 1989, when it was re-erected, a perfectly preserved engraving was discovered on its underside—a square with a crescent moon at its top right corner (*opposite*). The length of the crescent equals the diagonal of the square. Around 4000 BC, every 18.6 years, the northernmost moonrise was precisely north-east, at 45°. So, over a two week period, the rising and setting moon would have traced a square on the horizon, marking out the ordinal directions (NE, SE, SW, NW).

In a continuation of this geometry, the corridor of La Table des Marchands (*shown on page 88*) aligns the major southernmost moonrise over the Mane Er Hroëch and Le Petit Mont tumuli. Between these different monuments, a giant double square is traced whose diagonal (Grand Menhir – Kermaillard) marks the *minor* moon axis (*below*).

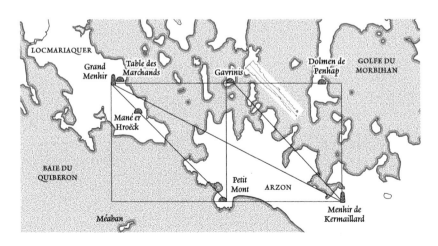

Above left: Another crescent moon and square on the rear (invisible) side of the ogival stone at the Table des Marchands dolmen in Locmariaquer. Right: Menhir de Kermillard.

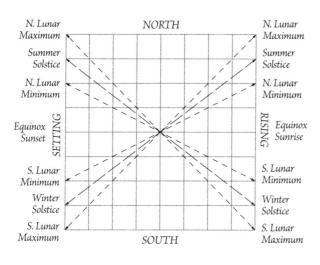

Left: An extension of the diagram of page 29. At the latitude of Carnac, all the extreme solar and lunar rising & setting positions occur either along the diagonal of a square (moon), or the diagonal of a 3-4 rectangle (sun), producing this mastergrid.

The Carnac Alignments
together but different

The 4km long Carnac alignments divides into three sections. From west to east these are: Le Menec, Kermario and Kerlescan–Le Petit Menec. The first section is composed of Le Menec West and Le Menec East. The third section is divided in two by the Auray to La Trinité main road and bridges two towns (hence its two names). There are gaps between each section and the directions they take are different. The largest stones, some over 4m tall, are found at the west of each section. They then get progressively smaller towards the east, until they fade out (there exceptions to this rule, an occasional "Giant" stone, and larger stones at the eastern end of the Le Menec rows).

At Le Menec and Kerlescan, a starting line is marked by touching menhirs perpendicular to the rows, part of a cromlech which encloses the plateau. There is no similar structure at the head of the Kermario Alignments showing that they are perhaps linked to Le Menec.

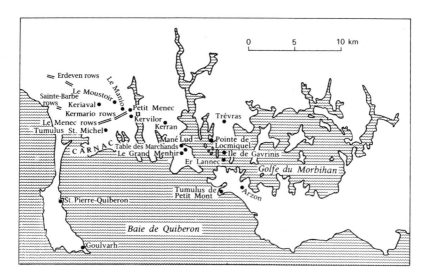

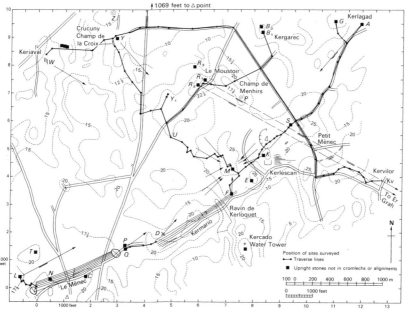

GEOLOGICAL CHARACTERISTICS
news from bedrock

A flat area of slightly higher ground with visible bedrock can be found at the start of all three series. Each line of stones starts on the eastern limit of this plateau and goes westwards down a slope. They then go up a bank to a central hillock, down the other side and then up a slope to the final plateau.

According to geological work by Dominique Sellier, many of the menhirs were "sliced" off the granite bedrock, as one face of the stone is harder than the other. The harder face was systematically orientated in the same direction. All the stones are roughly hewn, and although certain shapes recur, none are identical. They are similar to those at Avebury in Great Britain.

The study of vertical erosion on the granite suggests the "Le Menec giant" may date to 5000 BC, making it up to 2000 years older than its neighbours. If so, this would show incredible continuity at the site.

An important discovery was made in 1991: the alignments seem to follow the underlying fracturing of the bedrock (*shown opposite*).

Above: A semi-fanciful image of 20 rows of the Erdeven alignments, c.1870. Below: A study undertaken by EDF, the French electricity company, in 1991 using aerial photo-geological techniques showed, amazingly, that all the alignments follow the underlying fracturing of the bedrock, invisible to the naked eye. Also, at the westerly end of the alignments, Le Menec West, there is intense north-south fracturing. Magnetometer experiments gave results too anomalous to be published.

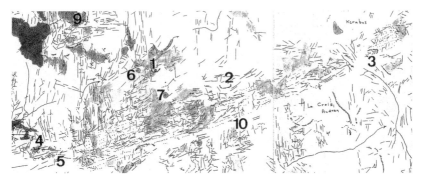

TUMULUS SAINT MICHEL

3 + 2 = 1

Dominating the whole of the Carnac area, the Tumulus Saint Michel is an artificial mound weighing around 67,000 tons, surmounted by a 17th century chapel. It crowns the summit of the highest natural hilltop in south Carnac and offers a 360° view to up to 40 km away. Measured by René Galles in 1862 as 115m long by 58m wide (a 1:2 ratio), its modern dimensions are 125m by 60m. Excavations have uncovered many Neolithic jadeite polished ritual axe heads.

The Tumulus' orientation is N18.5°E—the diagonal of a cardinal triple square (*centre, opposite*). The path which leads up to the top of the mound runs along the diagonal of the square and the double square. When extended, this line heads to the Kerlescan alignments, over 2km away. It also corresponds to the most northerly moonrise which happens every 18.6 years (*see too page 119*).

The Mané Lud tumulus (*see page 83*) at Locmariaquer, although lower in height, has exactly the same ground plan and orientation.

Left: Excavations uncovered a central chamber just 2.4 by 1.4m and 1m high, covered by a massive capstone with 6 cup marks engraved on the underside. A larger dolmen was discovered close to the eastern end of the tumulus.

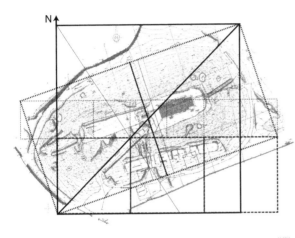

Left: The orientation of the Tumulus is given by the diagonal of a cardinal triple square. A double square born of the triple square encloses the Tumulus, and its diagonal then becomes the diagonal of a large single square: 18.435° + 26.565° = 45°. The overall width of this plan is 7 units, with the triple square measuring 6 x 2 and the large square having sides of 5.

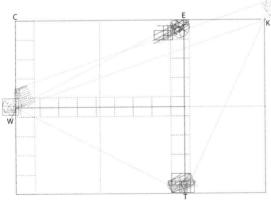

Left: Three double squares, two horizontal and one vertical, each precisely 450m x 900m oriented NSEW, combine into a 3 x 2 rectangle which positions the Kermario dolmen (K), the Tumulus Saint Michel (T), the start of row 11 at Le Menec West (W), the top and centre of the Le Menec East egg (E) and the Crifol menhir (C).

LE MENEC WEST
cromlech and alignments

The Le Menec West cromlech sits among houses in the Le Menec village. 71 stones remain, many touching, which reveal the original shape, verified in 19th century plans by Blair, Ronalds and Gaillard.

Professor Thom classified it as a Type-1 egg, based on two 3-4-5 triangles placed back to back (*see opposite*), also found in some stone "circles" in Britain. Thom suggested the megalithic yard (0.829m) as the core measurement of the megalith builders and its 2.5 multiple, the megalithic rod (mr). Thom did not realise that one side of his upper 3-4-5 triangle was orientated north-south. A circle drawn around the two 3-4-5 triangles has a well at its centre.

Another Pythagorean triangle hides in Thom's plan, the 7-24-25. The two smaller angles of the 3-4-5 triangle (36.87°) when added make 73.74°. If this is subtracted from 90°, we obtain 16.26° which is the angle of the 7-24-25 triangle. The 25 side measures 25mr, showing how this triangle has given the egg's dimensions.

Eleven lines then lead away from the cromlech, and form the Le Menec West alignments (*opposite*).

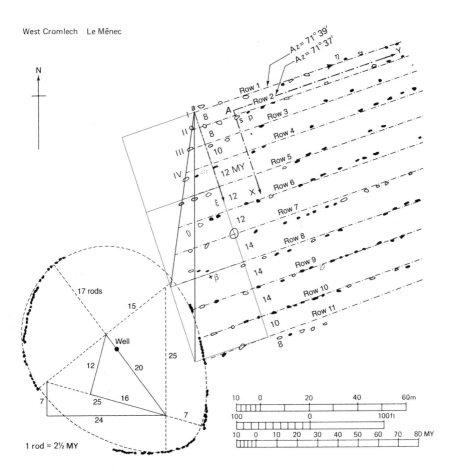

Above: *The Le Menec West cromlech and alignments. Thom noticed how the northerly menhirs (rows 1 to 5) are at a 1:2 angle, or 63.435°, with respect to the rows themselves, the diagonal of a double square, an alignment repeated as the rows progressed. The double square also shows how the sum of the four spaces between rows 1-5 (38 megalithic yards, 8+8+10+12) is the same as the sum of the three spaces between rows 5-8 (12+12+14 my). Rows 8-11 also add up to 38my (14+14+10), creating a triple square, whose diagonal is precisely orientated north-south. So the Le Menec alignments follow the direction of the diagonal of an east-west triple square, for about 400m until they come to the central hillock, where they mysteriously turn towards the north.*

LE MENEC EAST

from a triple to a double square

The Le Menec East alignments have their tallest stones to the east, so seem to be heading southwest (the opposite way to the other alignments). The line on Professor Thom's plan which goes through the most stones is row 7, for which he gives an angle of 26.55° north of East, the angle of the diagonal of a double square. However, Thom's overall interpretation of the Menec alignments (*shown below*) was not a huge success. For once, a megalithic site partially defeated him.

In fact, the rows at Le Menec East follow the same principles as at Le Menec West: the distance between rows 1-5 is 27my (6+7+7+7), the same as between rows 5-8 (9+9+9). As in the west, the sum of the first four gaps equals to that of the next three. The lower part of this site has unfortunately been destroyed by the road.

Since the angle of the rows is the diagonal of a northerly aligned double square, the 27my is shown opposite as the diagonal of a dotted double square. Lines 1, 5, 7 and 8, when extended, run to the stones on the north-east side of the cromlech. The side of the dotted square is north-south, so aligned along the meridian.

Until recently, the Tumulus Saint Michel was clearly visible due south of the head of these alignments.

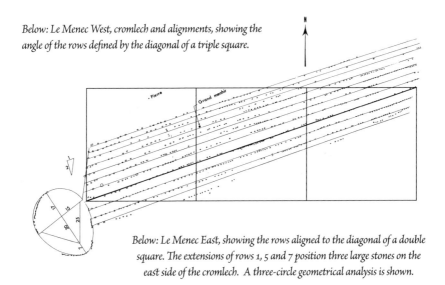

Below: Le Menec West, cromlech and alignments, showing the angle of the rows defined by the diagonal of a triple square.

Below: Le Menec East, showing the rows aligned to the diagonal of a double square. The extensions of rows 1, 5 and 7 position three large stones on the east side of the cromlech. A three-circle geometrical analysis is shown.

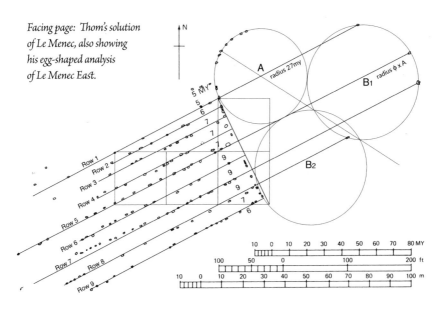

Facing page: Thom's solution of Le Menec, also showing his egg-shaped analysis of Le Menec East.

A System of Squares

building blocks to squeeze irrationals

There is an interesting summary of the geometry to be found at Le Menec. The two major directions of the lines are given by a septuple square. The western section runs along its sides while the diagonal positions the orientation of the eastern rows.

It is placed exactly between the two cromlechs and its diagonal measures precisely 950m. This gives each square a side length of 950 / $\sqrt{50}$ = 134.35m, a measurement used at the Tumulus Saint Michel. A solitary standing stone circled at the top of the first square on the left could well be a remaining marker of this geometry.

This method of arithmetical tracing gives exact angular results. The angle of the diagonal of a septuple square is 8.130°. At Le Menec we see how the diagonals of a triple square and a septuple square produce the double square (*top, opposite*): 18.435° + 8.130° = 26.565°

Also interesting is the fact that doubling the angle of a septuple square gives the angle of a 7-24-25 triangle, seen to have been the basis of the Le Menec West cromlech (*centre, opposite*): 8.130° x 2 = 16.260°

The angle of a septuple square also relates the 3-4-5 triangle and the square (*lower, opposite*): 36.87° + 8.13° = 45°

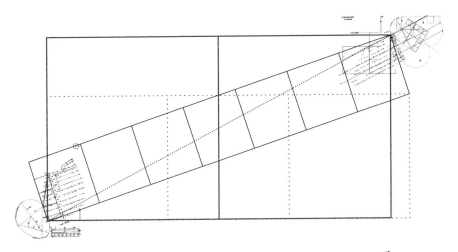

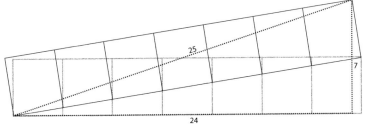

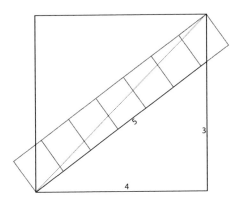

Top: A geometrical composite overview of the Le Menec alignments. The Carnac builders were fascinated by simple square grids. Double squares, triple squares, and even septuple squares are hidden much of their work.

Centre: A double septuple square produces a 7-24-25 rectangle.

Left: A septuple square connects a square and a 3-4-5 rectangle

LE MENEC TO KERMARIO
the middle alignments

To the East of Le Menec can be found the Kermario rows. These seem to initially curve, but are in fact a succession of straight lines which slightly change direction at certain points. Their start is an extension of the Le Menec West lines, 1.4km away (the diagonal of a triple square, 18.435° north of east), with the most southerly row (11) at Le Menec West running towards the Kermario dolmen and the other rows at Le Menec West all linking to those at the beginning of Kermario. The most northerly line, row 1, continues the furthest before changing direction, the while at the dolmen, to the south, the change of direction is immediate. The full scheme is shown in the two diagrams (*opposite*).

There are eleven rows at Kermario, and they finally run at an angle 33.7° north of east, the diagonal of a 2×3 rectangle (*shown on page 109*).

Fig. 49. — KERMARIO (Propriété de l'État). Vue prise de l'Est avant la restauration
Ensemble d'une avenue des alignements du commencement de Kermario. — Dix alignements.

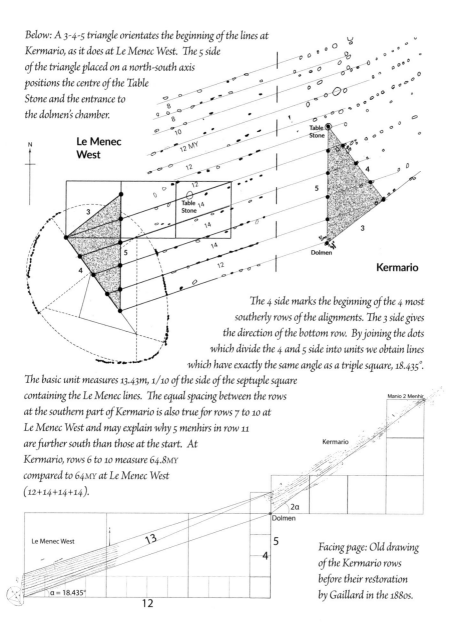

Below: A 3-4-5 triangle orientates the beginning of the lines at Kermario, as it does at Le Menec West. The 5 side of the triangle placed on a north-south axis positions the centre of the Table Stone and the entrance to the dolmen's chamber.

Le Menec West

N

Table Stone

Kermario

Dolmen

The 4 side marks the beginning of the 4 most southerly rows of the alignments. The 3 side gives the direction of the bottom row. By joining the dots which divide the 4 and 5 side into units we obtain lines which have exactly the same angle as a triple square, 18.435°.

The basic unit measures 13.43m, 1/10 of the side of the septuple square containing the Le Menec lines. The equal spacing between the rows at the southern part of Kermario is also true for rows 7 to 10 at Le Menec West and may explain why 5 menhirs in row 11 are further south than those at the start. At Kermario, rows 6 to 10 measure 64.8MY compared to 64MY at Le Menec West (12+14+14+14).

Manio 2 Menhir

Kermario

2α

Dolmen

Le Menec West

13

5

4

α = 18.435°

12

Facing page: Old drawing of the Kermario rows before their restoration by Gaillard in the 1880s.

KERMARIO

rows by any other name would be so fair

An astounding global geometry appears in the complex Kermario system. The major axis of the alignments is 33.69° north of east. It can be measured exactly between the Table Stone and the 4m tall Le Manio 2 menhir near their eastern end. This is the precise angle of the diagonal of a 2 by 3 rectangle (*see opposite*).

Between the entrance to the dolmen's chamber and Le Manio 2 is a line, marked by the most southerly row of stones and certain stones near the middle of the alignments, which is at an angle of N53.13°E or 36.87° north of east, the angle of a 3-4-5 triangle. When extended, it positions the corner of the Kerlescan cromlech. The 4 side is on the E-W line leading to the Kercado Tumulus. The Table Stone and the dolmen are in a perfect N-S relationship.

The 2×3 rectangle and the 3-4-5 triangle consequently share the same East-West measurement. If we divide this side into 12 units, our 3-4-5 triangle becomes a 9-12-15 and our 2×3 rectangle an 8×12. So the rectangle has 8 units on the North-South axis and the triangle has 9. The distance between the Table Stone and the dolmen is thus 1 unit. A GPS device with a precision of 1cm gives the measurements between the different points.

The diagonal of a 2×3 rectangle is $\sqrt{(2^2+3^2)} = \sqrt{13}$. So the distance between the dolmen and Le Manio 2 is $15 \times 1000/(\sqrt{13} \times 4) = 1040.06$.

We can conclude that the geometry was implemented to perfection, using exact angles with respect to the precise cardinal directions.

STONES & FRAGMENTS BELONGING TO THE LINES AT KERMARIO.

Above: Some of the stones of Kermario as drawn by Blair and Ronalds in 1832.
Below: Diagram showing the precise geometry and metrology of the Kermario alignments.

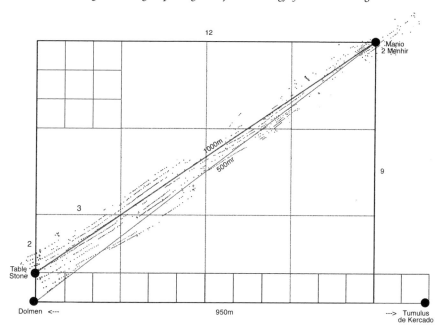

THE KERCADO TUMULUS
scales or whales

---

950 metres due east of the Kermario dolmen, on the highest point in the area, lies the magical 4680 BC Kercado Tumulus, thought to be one of the most ancient monuments in the area (the menhir on its summit is a recent addition). It is incredibly well preserved. Around its base are the remaining 27 stones of a circle, the tallest of which (1.6m) marks the corridor's axis. Others show weathering that confirms their great age.

Inside, a 6m long corridor, orientated along the diagonal of a triple square, leads to a 3m deep chamber with a massive coverstone, which, as at Gavrinis, rests on the stones in the cairn. It has a remarkable engraving of a plough/scales/whale (*shown opposite, and see similar engravings from the Mane Ruthual dolmen at Locmariaquer, below*). Engravings on several uprights are of a geometrical nature, one in particular clearly showing a sevenfold square (*see pages 99 and 105*).

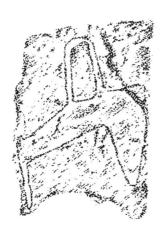 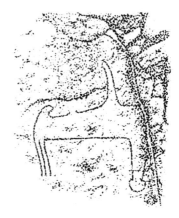

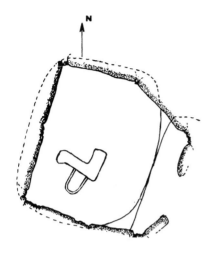

Left: The dolmen chamber and coverstone inside the Kercado Tumulus, showing engraving underneath. A full scale cardboard reproduction was shown to be in balance around the centre of the "handle", the vertical mass on the right being an exact counterweight to the horizontal left-hand side. The design may symbolise the weighing of souls, well-known in ancient Egypt, the balance between materialistic (horizontal) and spiritual (vertical) actions.

Below: General plan of the Kercado Tulumus (from AAK, Association Archéologique Kergal).

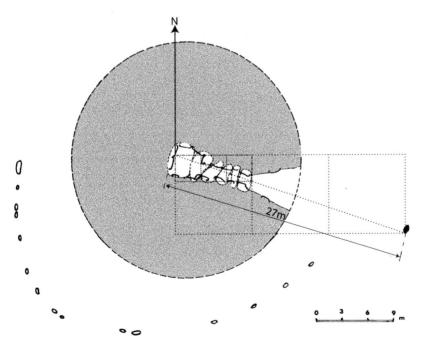

KERLESCAN CROMLECHS
west is west

There are many monuments at Kerlescan, some restored, but the best known are the alignments with a cromlech to the west. The cromlech lies on a plateau and is a perfect spot for astronomical observation although woodland now makes this difficult. It is square-shaped with its west side curved. To the north, there are no stones but there are the remains of a long, low mound which apparently pre-dates the cromlech. Several very low stones were used as an enclosure to this mound, but they are in no way part of the cromlech. The mound has a 3.5m tall menhir at its western end. 100m further north, the remains of another cromlech still exist. It must have been enormous and oval shaped originally but it is unfortunately now buried in woodland.

The southern side of the cromlech can be seen to have withstood the effects of millennia. All of its stones were still standing in 1870. The cromlech's height and width are equal, so it is a square orientated North-South. Its diagonal aims at the Tumulus Saint Michel.

Many of the large stones on the east side of the plateau are now touching each other but 13 out of 20 stones have been re-erected. Five stones at the centre of this line were still standing in 1870 and it can be seen that they are orientated along a perfect N-S axis.

Above: The Kerlescan plateau and cromlech drawn by Blair and Ronalds in 1832. In the foreground can be seen the fallen stones on the limit of the plateau. These are perpendicular to the alignments.

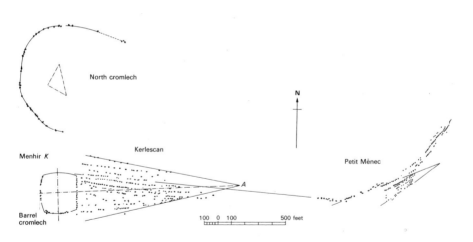

Above: The general plan of the Kerlescan megalithic complex. To the north is a massive open stone curve over 200m across. To the east the Le Petit Menec alignments form the arc of a vast circle.

KERLESCAN ALIGNMENTS
east is east

Twelve rows go downhill eastwards from the plateau and converge at a point approximately 370m from the cromlech, 180 mr according to Thom, on the crest of the following hill. The point of convergence, O, is situated in the village of Kerlescan.

There is an E-W axis, perpendicular to the side of the cromlech, which is the basis for the rows' angles. From point O, the E-W line goes through many standing stones, the first group being just south of the track. Further west, as it crosses row 6, the stones change angle to run along it. Then it touches the north side of the Kerlescan index stone, a massive block of granite between rows 7 and 8, much bigger than the surrounding stones. When viewed from the west, it has a curve on the top left. At equinox sunrise, on the 21st March and the 23rd September, an observer positioned on a mound near the west side of the cromlech sees the sunrise due east along the E-W axis and then, as the Sun climbs into the sky, it rolls in a groove on the curved edge of the index stone for about 15 minutes until it "takes off" from the stone's summit. The use of the 3-4-5 triangle and the septuple square can be seen in the layout of the central rows.

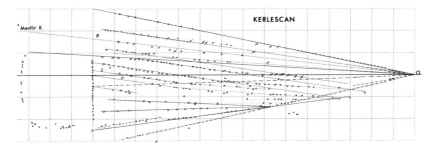

Above : The detailed plan of the Stones at Kerlescan (Thom) showing how the lines converge to a point. There is however a more complex geometry in the central section (see below).

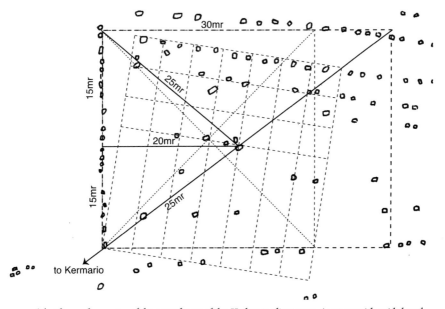

The plan and geometry of the central part of the Kerlescan alignments. A square with a side length of 30 megalithic rods, marked by the North-South line to the east of the cromlech and with the index stone at its centre, seems to have been turned by the angle of a septuple square to create a new square (marked by the dotted lines). The diagonal of this new square indicates the solstice angle and creates a 3×4 rectangle, the centre of which is also marked by a massive stone.

LE PETIT MENEC
curves and tangents

A calm shaded footpath between dry stone walls heads east from the village of Kerlescan, crosses the main road from Auray to La Trinité and leads us, just on the other side, to the alignments known as Le Petit Menec. No massive stones are to be found here. It is nothing like the start of Le Menec, Kermario or Kerlescan. Of course, the building of the road has seriously perturbed this section, but even so there can be very little doubt that this is not the beginning of a new series of alignments but the continuation of the Kerlescan site. These alignments are not closed to the public by fencing and offer an extremely pleasant and shaded visit on a hot summer afternoon.

The first few stones, on either side of the path after the road, are more or less E-W. Then, there are three major sections in this monument which correspond to three different orientations, turning progressively north.

	Section 1	Section 2	Section 3
Slope	1:3	4:7	1:1
Angle from East	18.435°	29.75°	45°
E-W length	63m	98m	77m

The continual process by which the alignments turn towards the north would suggest the curve as general outline to these rows. These alignments are in fact tracing a circle with a 343m radius using tangents (*lower, opposite*). One sixth part of the circle is shown here and it corresponds exactly to the length of the alignments.

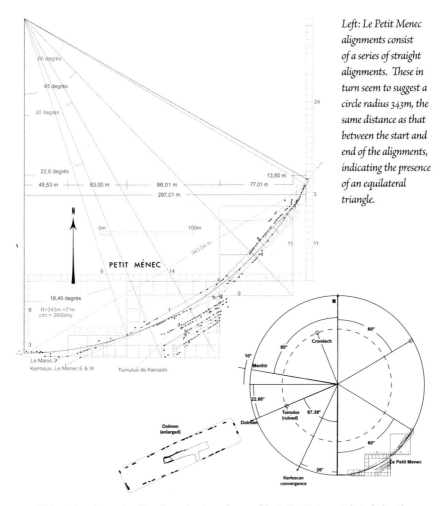

Left: Le Petit Menec alignments consist of a series of straight alignments. These in turn seem to suggest a circle radius 343m, the same distance as that between the start and end of the alignments, indicating the presence of an equilateral triangle.

Right: Many interesting things lie on the circumference of the Le Petit Menec circle, including the Kerlescan dolmen, whose southern kerb points straight to the centre of the circle on the exact angle of a NSEW 5-12-13 triangle. Along this line, a ruined tumulus seems to indicate the existence of an inner circle, whose presence is supported by a mound and cromlech 90° clockwise around the perimeter. A well-known standing stone, about 3 metres high is also found close to the circumference north of the dolmen.

A General Plan
planetary geometry and measurement

Is there a general plan underlying the positioning of these massive megalithic monuments? If we look at the relationship between the tumulus Saint Michel and Le Grand Menhir, the two most important sites in the area, we discover a relationship based on the quintuple square (*shown below*), the exact angle running from the central chamber in the tumulus to the menhir. The precise distance is 9444.4 m which gives a side length for each square of 1852.2 m, the exact value of the nautical mile (one minute of arc of the Earth's meridian; 1852.2 x 60 x 360 = 40,007,520m). The East-West distance between the two monuments is 5 nautical miles or 9261m which is $7^3 \times 3^3$m. Could such precision be a coincidence, and if not, what does this imply?

Le Menec and Kermario are linked by a triple square, and Kermario and Kerlescan by a 3-4-5 triangle, so the angle with respect to east is doubled: $18.435° \times 2 = 36.87°$. The Tumulus Saint Michel is at the centre of an array of monuments positioned according to the major and minor risings and settings of the Moon. This incredible plan links together all the natural hilltops.

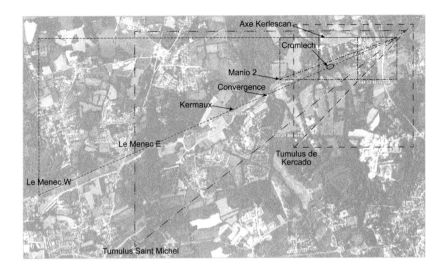

Labels on image 1: Axe Kerlescan, Cromlech, Manio 2, Convergence, Kermaux, Le Menec E, Le Menec W, Tumulus de Kercado, Tumulus Saint Michel

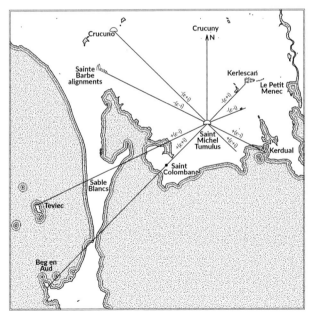

Labels on image 2: Crucuno, Crucuny, N, Sainte Barbe alignments, Kerlescan, Le Petit Menec, Saint Michel Tumulus, Kerdual, Saint Colomban, Sable Blancs, Teviec, Beg en Aud

Above: By extending the lines in the different sections at Le Petit Menec, the major monuments of Carnac can be positioned.

Left: The different monuments at extreme lunar rising and setting positions around the Tumulus Saint Michel (illustrated page 98).

Opposite: The diagonal of a pentuple square precisely connects the Tumulus Saint Michel and the Grand Menhir.

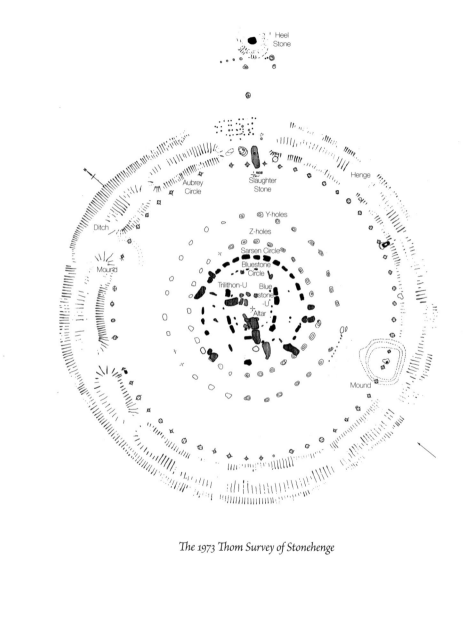

The 1973 Thom Survey of Stonehenge

STONEHENGE

Robin Heath

18 CASTLE RIGG
19 LONG MEG
20 SWINSIDE
1 CALLANISH
2 BROGAR
3 CLAVA
17 PENMAENMAWR
4 ARBOR LOW
16 PIPERS
5 BAR BROOK
15 MOEL TY UCHAF
6 AVEBURY
14 GORS FAWR
7 STONEHENGE
13 MERRIVALE
12 MERRY MAIDENS
11 BOSCAWEN UN
10 HURLERS
9 ROUGH TOR
8 STANTON DREW

Principle Stone Circles of the British Isles

INTRODUCTION

Stonehenge is Britain's national temple. Attracting almost one million visitors a year, the monument, now a World Heritage Site, has become the country's most visited tourist attraction. Yet, despite its popularity, this prehistoric monument remains shrouded in mystery and still provokes many questions in both layman and specialist alike—who built it, when, and for what purposes? Why were all those huge stones moved such unfeasibly long distances to then become placed so precisely?

These questions remained largely unanswered until fairly recently, and this book charts the emergence of Stonehenge into the collective modern psyche, from naive medieval speculations to modern scientific methodology and New Age revelations.

When accurate techniques of radiocarbon dating became available in the late 1960s, the dating for the original monument was pushed back over 1000 years, to before 3000 BC. This cleft an embarrassing split in the archeological record, the construction of Stonehenge being initiated before the Great Pyramid and almost every other megalithic building in the ancient world (*megalith* is Greek for 'large stone'). The previously held idea that civilisation and culture had gradually diffused from the Middle East became untenable. An apparently safe archaeological paradigm, diffusionism, collapsed.

Interestingly, at precisely this same time, the astronomy, metrology and geometry of Stonehenge and many other stone circles was being revealed, not always with the blessing or agreement of orthodox archaeologists.   A lively ferment of debate between archaeologists and astronomers, historians and engineers initiated, in the early 70s, a most creative period of reassessment for Stonehenge and its original purpose.

Stonehenge is far more than just an impressive display of huge stones. If it were merely that, it would fail to maintain such a powerful presence within our present culture.   Up to 40,000 people arrive each year in the hope of observing the midsummer sunrise from the monument.   Stonehenge is a symbol or icon of *Albion*, the ancient wisdom of Britain and of different cultural values from a vanished time.   Using Stonehenge as a lens, we can truly see into the mind of a Neolithic architect and thereby connect back to our prehistoric ancestors. To what did they aspire?

As we begin a new millennium, Stonehenge's sixth, the apparently disparate subjects of archaeology, astronomy, metrology and sacred geometry are slowly converging to reveal a holistic Megalithic Science.

Once part of an impressively large collection of stone circles throughout northwestern Europe, Stonehenge, with its raised circle of lintels yet differs from all the rest.   Unique, and having survived five millennia and several cultural changes, Stonehenge is a Stone Age cathedral, the centrepiece of a once wealthy and evidently learned tribal community.   Their magnificent legacy of stone beckons us to read its message.

DIGGING IN THE DARK
the rediscovery of Stonehenge

Ever since the end of the Dark Ages, descriptions and illustrations of Stonehenge have been interwoven with the cultural fantasies of the time—so remote is the culture which built the monument. In 1655, Inigo Jones, architect to King James I, added a sixth trilithon to link Stonehenge to Roman styles (*see below*). The Age of the Antiquarian dawned in the 1670s with John Aubrey, and later William Stukeley; Stonehenge now became 'temple plus druids'.

Plundering of this and other ancient sites followed. A notorious duo, Richard Colt-Hoare and William Cunningham, practiced reverse alchemy—replacing struck gold found in nearby burial barrows with dull lead tokens. In those days, archaeology was undertaken with pick-axe and shovel, and much irrevocable damage was done, and invaluable evidence irretrievably lost.

More recently, Colonel Hawley, William Flinders-Petrie, Norman Lockyer and professors Richard Atkinson, Gerald Hawkins and Alexander Thom pioneered new approaches to understanding those 'immemorial gray pillars'.

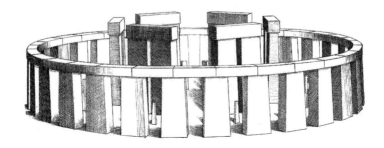

A The Stones call'd Corsstones, 12 Tonn Weight
24 foot high, 7 broad, and 16 round
B The Stones call'd Coronetts, of 6 or 7 Tonns
C The place where Mens bones are dug up.

Above: A bizarre and inaccurate engraving of Stonehenge from William Camden's Britannia, 1607, a highly popular topographical and historical survey of Great Britain and Ireland, that placed Stonehenge in front of a much wider public.

THE STONEHENGE LANDSCAPE
the remains on the plain

Stonehenge forms the centrepiece of a rich heritage on Salisbury Plain. Within a few miles of the monument can be found mesolithic postholes dating to 8000 BC, two unexplained cursuses (long rectangular swathes of land enclosed by embanked sides, dating to 3600 BC and 3000 BC), several long barrows (c.3500 BC), Woodhenge (2400 BC, *see page 160*), a 2000 foot embanked linear Avenue (c.2500 BC) leading from Stonehenge to the River Avon, many single standing stones and various types of barrows attributed to the later Wessex culture (2000–1400 BC, *marked •* *in the Ordnance Survey map opposite*).

The impressive Stonehenge cursus is over two miles long and averages 420 feet in width, enclosing over 100 acres of land. It has variously been described as a UFO runway, tornado strip or jousting arena. It was probably none of these, although why would anyone wish to construct such a strange alignment, especially so near to Stonehenge itself? Stukeley's 1740 engraving of the cursus is shown below.

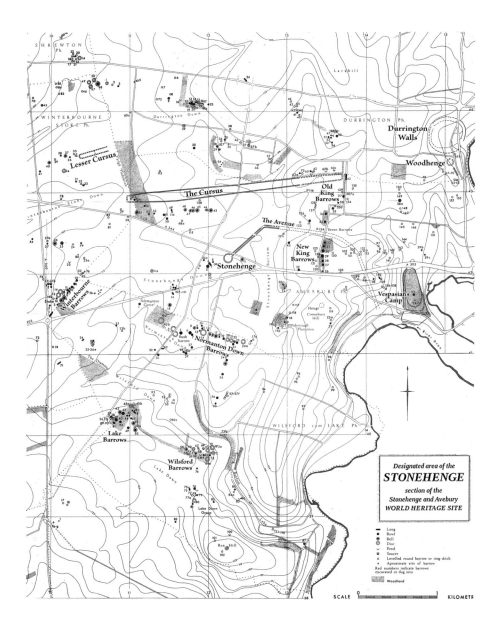

Designated area of the
STONEHENGE
section of the
Stonehenge and Avebury
WORLD HERITAGE SITE

Long
Bowl
Bell
Disc
Pond
Saucer
Levelled round barrow or ring-ditch
Aproximate site of barrow
Red numbers indicate barrows
excavated or dug into

Woodland

SCALE 0   KILOMETR

TRAVELS TO THE OTHERWORLD
a culture of life after death

The Stonehenge landscape includes many examples of what are known as barrows (*opposite, from Richard Colt Hoare, 1812*). Many of these contained burials or cremated remains. The artefacts interred alongside the dead have provided archaeologists with much information about social patterns within the Wessex Culture. The foetal position of many of the skeletons suggests a rebirth from within Mother Earth. Many burial chambers throughout the entire megalithic culture are aligned to the midwinter sunrise or sunset, supporting such a theory, the symbolism being that, at the shortest days of midwinter, the 'death' of the Sun thereafter leads to its resurrection, a daily increase in light, strength and noonday height, as each sunrise and sunset occurs more to the north.

An recent excavation at Stonehenge unearthed the skeleton of an archer, with arrowheads still lodged in his vertebrae. Ritual sacrifice, execution or murder? We will probably never know.

1. LONG BARROW.

3. BELL BARROW.   2. BOWL BARROW.

4. DRUID BARROW.

STONEHENGE CULTURE
artefacts from the past

What little we know about the people who built Stonehenge has traditionally come from archaeology. Accurate radiocarbon dating techniques have greatly assisted this process. Local museums in Salisbury and Devizes display wonderful treasures taken from the earth here. Fine gold artefacts, polished maces, riveted sword-hafts, flint arrowheads and elegant pottery contrast with crude stone maul hammers, arthritic bones and low life-expectancy.

Polished mace and axe-heads (*below*) date from 2500BC and are often made from semi-precious stones. Fine flat-bottomed beaker folk pottery (circa 2300BC), finely knapped arrowheads and an exquisitely decorated ceremonial bronze axehead from 2000 BC (*all illustrated opposite*) reveal a culture whose functional priorities were matched by artistic expertise. These people were not savages!

It is worthwhile imagining how such people could equip, feed and organise the labourers who undertook Dr Gerald Hawkins' estimated twelve million man-hours needed to construct Stonehenge, their finest artefact.

  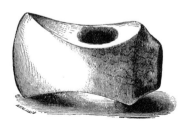

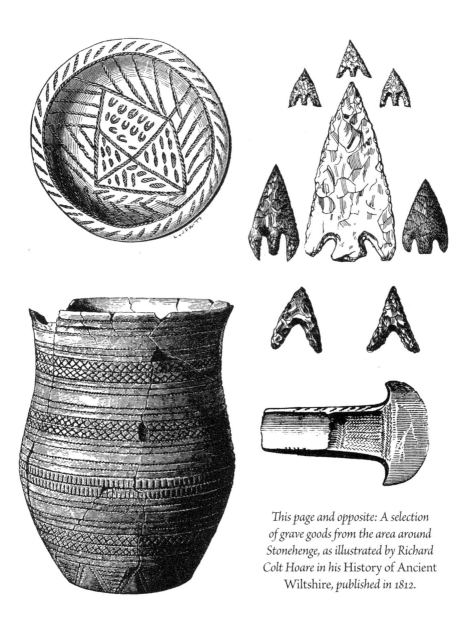

This page and opposite: A selection of grave goods from the area around Stonehenge, as illustrated by Richard Colt Hoare in his History of Ancient Wiltshire, published in 1812.

BARROWLOADS OF GOLD
a ninefold astronomical lozenge

At the Bush Barrow, an early Bronze Age site just south of Stonehenge, Stukeley found nothing, while Cunningham, in 1808, plundered his finest treasure—the Bush Barrow 'lozenge'.

Lying over the breast of a tall man, this exquisite artefact, made from beaten gold, was once mounted on a wooden plate, and measures 7 inches in length (*shown opposite*). Bronze rivets mixed with wood and thin strips of bronze were interred nearby. The lozenge may today be viewed at the Devizes Museum.

The internal angles of the lozenge are 82° and 98°. Keith Critchlow proposed a nine-fold geometry (80° and 100°) supporting the nine triangles along each side and the central diamond of nine smaller diamonds. A more accurate solution by Anthony Johnson involves a hexagonal solution (*opposite top right*). Uniquely at the latitude of Stonehenge, the extreme range of sunrises and sets occurs over an 81° span of the horizon, and those of the Moon over 102° (*opposite lower right and left*). This has led some researchers to suggest that the lozenge was a sighting device and the tall man an astronomer-priest. Astronomical significance or not, the lozenge supplies firm evidence of advanced craft skills and a refined knowledge of geometry in the area around Stonehenge.

The man was also buried with two metal daggers, a bronze axe, a lance-head, a second smaller gold lozenge, a gold belt-hook, a stone mace-head and decorated bone ornaments. In fact, not at all the normal tackle of a modern astronomer!

THE BUSHBARROW LOZENGE
Normanton Down
1900-1700 BC

0   5cm

ASTRONOMY & GEOMETRY
a prehistoric culture of circle builders

In 1973 Alexander Thom undertook the first accurate survey of Stonehenge (*see frontispiece*). Having previously surveyed over 500 stone circles, he confirmed that a unit of 2.72 feet (0.829m) had been used by their builders, which he called the Megalithic yard.

A third of Thom's surveyed stone circles were actually not circles at all, and their geometry derives from Pythagorean triangles often in whole numbers of Megalithic yards and probably laid out with rope and pegs. Some examples are shown here—note how often the key points are marked by a stone. Some 'circles', such as Castlerigg (*opposite top left*), have their geometry aligned to key astronomical rising and setting positions of Sun, Moon and stars, as does Stonehenge. Horizon landscape features were also often skillfully incorporated. Why were ancient astronomers applying Pythagorean geometry over 2000 years before Pythagoras was born?

Recently a Type I Egg was discovered at Nabta, in the Sudan (*see page 50*). It has been dated at 4500BC, sited in time and space well away from the previously held boundaries of megalithic circle builders.

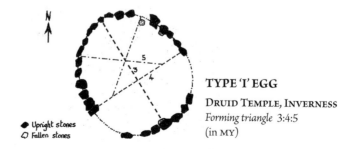

● Upright stones
◌ Fallen stones

TYPE 'I' EGG
DRUID TEMPLE, INVERNESS
Forming triangle 3:4:5
(in MY)

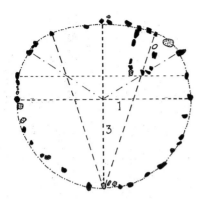

TYPE 'A' FLATTENED CIRCLE

CASTLERIGG, KESWICK, CUMBRIA
Forming triangle 1:3:√10
Diameter 40 MY

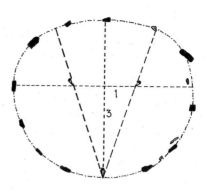

TYPE 'B' FLATTENED CIRCLE

BARBROOK, DERBYSHIRE
Forming triangle 1:3:√10
(in units of 3 MY)

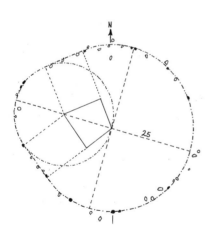

TYPE 'II' EGG

BORROWSTON RIG, SCOTS BORDERS
Forming triangle 3:4:5
Diameter 50 MY

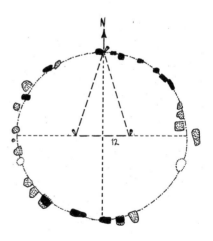

ELLIPSE

DAVIOT 'B', ABERDEENSHIRE
Forming triangle 12:35:37
(in units of ¼ MY)

The First Stonehenge
an implosion over 1500 years

Stonehenge's concentric circles of stones and postholes evolved inwards with time - the very opposite of a raindrop falling on water. This implosion evolved over 1500 years.

The circular outer ditch and bank, once 6 foot high, is dated to around 3150 BC (*opposite top*). The axis entrance, flanked by the then upright 'slaughter stone' and a long gone companion stone, was filled with many experimental posts, apparently to monitor the most northerly moonrises each month (*opposite centre*), particularly the extreme midwinter moonrise which only occurs every eighteen years and seven months.

The entrance was later widened and the angle changed to that of the midsummer sunrise (*opposite bottom*). The Heel Stone, 'moated' within a small circular ditch marked the start of an 1800 foot long avenue, as shown on the extreme right of the upper illustration opposite. Stonehenge, predominantly a lunar observatory in its early phases, apparently became more a solar observatory as it evolved. Evidence for soli-lunar observations, eclipse prediction and the development of an accurate calendar also exists.

The name 'Heel Stone' perhaps derives from the Welsh or Greek word for Sun, *haul* and *helios* respectively. Its other popular name 'Friar's Heel', is thought to refer to an indent on the stone which resembles a heel-print. However, *ffriw yr haul* is phonetically almost identical, being the Old Welsh for 'appearance of the Sun', a far more apt reason for the name.

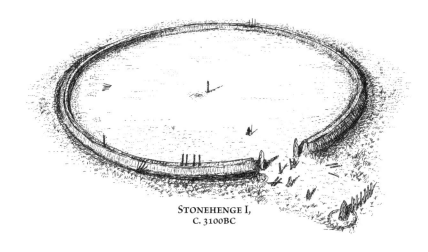

STONEHENGE I,
C. 3100BC

MOST NORTHERLY MOONRISE

MIDSUMMER SUNRISE

THE AUBREY CIRCLE
the number is 56

Named after antiquarian John Aubrey, who discovered them in 1676, the Aubrey Circle consists of 56 holes that form a very accurate circle with a mean diameter of 283.6 feet. This dimension connects through geometry and metrology to many of the later constructions at Stonehenge. Curiously, these holes were dug into the chalk subsoil around 3100BC, yet filled in only a century or two afterwards. Until recently, there has been no evidence as to why.

Were wooden posts, even a wooden henge monument, once placed in these holes or did they once define the first stone circle erected at the site? Recent research indicates that the Aubrey holes may have once held a circle of bluestones. Archaeologists have accounted for over 80 bluestones within later structures at Stonehenge, more than enough to fill the Aubrey holes.

In 1923, geologist H. H. Thomas discovered that the bluestones originated from outcrops in the Preseli mountains in Pembrokeshire, Wales, some 135 miles from Stonehenge. How they got to Salisbury plain remains somewhat contentious, some experts preferring glacial over human action. If only archaeologists could discover the remains of a prehistoric boat, sledge or rollers!

This raises a more interesting question. Why were the bluestones so important to this monument, so much so that they were employed in monumental constructions throughout all phases of Stonehenge's evolution?

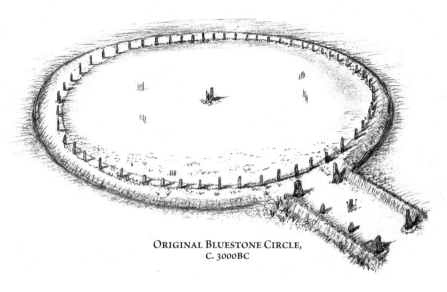

ORIGINAL BLUESTONE CIRCLE,
C. 3000BC

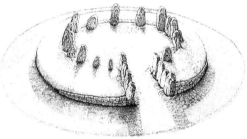

MEINI GWYR, PRESELI, WALES

*Above: Stonehenge's baby cousin. Meini Gwyr's
bluestones once framed an entrance that faced the
midsummer sunrise. 'Vicariously' dated to 2300 BC*

*Right: Stone 68 is one of several polished monoliths
with grooves, tenons or mortise 'cups' carved in them.*

GROOVED BLUESTONE

THE STATION STONE RECTANGLE
the dawning of a new era

Sometime around 2800 BC, a bluestone prototype henge monument was erected in the centre of the henge. Large post holes suggest this was a double semi-circular structure, erected in the form shown (*opposite top*). Furthermore, two bluestone have mortise holes, and several others on the Stonehenge have (or once had) tenons cut into their tops or grooves in their sides.

In the 1950s, Richard Atkinson excavated a 'bluestone layer' of chippings at Stonehenge, and suggested that the bluestones and their joints had been fabricated on-site. Other archaeologists have since suggested that an original henge monument was shipped stone by undressed stone from the Preseli Hills in West Wales, for unspecified reasons, and then dressed and polished on-site.

Very soon afterwards, this structure was dismantled off-site, and four sarsen uprights, known as the Station Stones, were set into an accurate 5:12 rectangle *just inside* the perimeter of the Aubrey Circle.

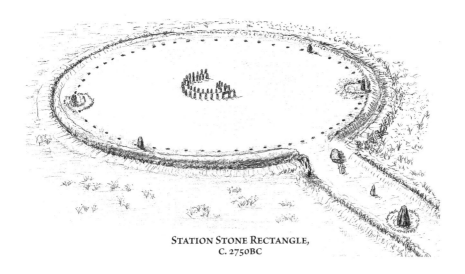

STATION STONE RECTANGLE,
C. 2750BC

Above: Stonehenge around 2750 BC.

Facing Page: Two of the Station Stones were placed on newly constructed mounds, one is visible in Richard Colt Hoare's engraving.

Right: The Station Stones form a Pythagorean 5:12:13 triangle whose dimensions are close to being 40, 96 and 104 MY. The Station Stones rectangle and its component Pythagorean triangles have remarkable properties relating to solar and lunar astronomy, but only near the latitude of Stonehenge. (For more detail see pages 157 and 174-175.)

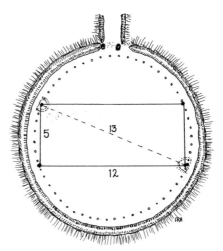

THE 5-12-13 PYTHAGOREAN
TRIANGLE, IN UNITS OF 8 MY
C. 2750BC

SARSENS & TRILITHONS
prehistoric monsters from a Neolithic past

Around 2600 BC the famous Sarsen Circle was constructed. Built on sloping ground, 30 uprights were crowned with a perfectly level circle of 30 raised sarsen stone lintels (*see opposite*). Five massive inner trilithons were also erected, of which three stand today. As the leviathan trilithon stones do not fit through the gaps in the Sarsen Circle, they were probably erected first. The sarsens were brought from Fyfield Down, 17 miles directly to the north of Stonehenge.

The Sarsen Circle was dressed on the stones' inner faces, and once supported a complete circle of thirty lintels about 15 feet above the ground. The trilithons were more finely dressed, yet curiously one of each pair of uprights was left rough. The five trilithons varied in height from 17 to 25 feet. The diameter of the Sarsen Circle through the centreline of the lintels is 100.8 feet. The elliptical trilithon 'horseshoe' measures 40 by 70 feet.

Sarsen is a sandstone several times harder than granite, and was dressed on site using sarsen mauls, weighing up to 63lb. Over 1800 of these have been excavated, many used as backfill after the upright stones had been placed into their positions.

Prior to this mammoth undertaking the earlier bluestone henge was dismantled and, centuries later, rearranged within the Sarsen Circle as an inner circle of 59 or 60 stones, about 75 feet in diameter, and a 39 foot diameter horseshoe of nineteen slender and polished bluestones, averaging 9 feet tall. Finally, the dressed 13 foot altar stone completed the edifice (*see plan on page 147*).

THE SARSEN CIRCLE

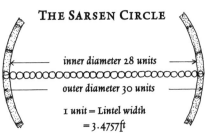

inner diameter 28 units

outer diameter 30 units

1 unit = Lintel width
= 3.4757ft

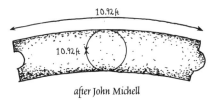

10.92 ft

10.92 ft

after John Michell

DIMENSIONS:

'Jewish' Sacred Rod = 3.4757ft
= Polar Radius / 6,000,000

Outer diameter = 30 sacred rods
= 104.27ft
Outer circumference = 327.58ft
Outer lintel length = 327.6 / 30
= 10.92ft

Inner diameter = 28 sacred rods
= 97.32ft
Inner circumference = 305.74ft
Inner lintel length = 10.19ft

Lintel width = 3.4757ft
= outer lintel length / π
= 10.92 / π

THE MIDDLE GROUND
the stones at the centre

With around a million visitors a year, Stonehenge is the world's most popular megalithic site. Today, to walk inside the central area requires 'special access' from the custodians, English Heritage.

The plan shown opposite, of the central area, is from Edgar Barclay's book *Stonehenge and its Earthworks*, published in 1895. Apart from the fallen trilithon (stones 57, 58 and lintel 158) which was re-erected in 1958, this plan is very similar to what we see today. Barclay used a numbering system devised by Flinders Petrie in the 1870s, the standard classification to this day. Of particular interest is stone 11, the half-width sarsen upright; stone 150, a bluestone with mortise holes; and stone 68, the grooved bluestone (*see page 141*).

Shown also is stone 156, the trilithon lintel curiously mortised on both sides. Was this an error made by the builders, or was there once a further construction aloft this highest platform at Stonehenge? Perhaps the structure supported a wooden roof, now long-rotted, to keep young astronomer-priests dry on wet nights.

North

25
26
127
27
28
29
30

Sarsen
Circle

Bluestone Circle

23
45
46
47
48
1

22
43
60   Trilithon-U
49
2

42
44
72   Bluestone-U
71
31

21
58
160 A
3

158
59
160 B
150
32

120
70
59
59
160 c
4

19
69
156
S.S.

57
67
80
61
S.

41
68
Altar stone
51
5

56
55 B
62
63
52
33

66
65
64
53
6

55 A
54
7

16
15
40
39
38
37
36
35 A
34
8

14
35 B

12
11
10
9 A
9 B

Axis

C

Sarsens in Situ.
„   recumbent.
Blue stones in Situ.
„   „   recumbent.
Horn stones
Soft schist stump
Altar stone

Scale, 1/200 or 6 inches = 100 feet.

WOODWORK IN STONE
how to do joined up megaliths

In order to fix the lintels, they were locked together like pieces of a jigsaw, using tongues and grooves. In addition, each upright was dressed with two tenons which mated with corresponding mortises on the lintels (*see below*). The visitor may still observe the tenons on many sarsen uprights where the lintels have fallen. These jointing techniques derive from the wood joiner's craft and were also applied to bluestone lintels, thought to be part of a now demolished bluestone trilithon structure. A mortise hole on Stone 150 remains visible, while those on the underside of Stone 36, reburied following inspection, remain hidden underground.

The mighty trilithon uprights carried a large single tenon and their lintels were duly mortised. The tallest stone (56) still sports its tenon, like a jockey's cap thrown up as a prank, whilst its twin (Stone 55) and the curiously double-mortised lintel (Stone 156) have long since fallen.

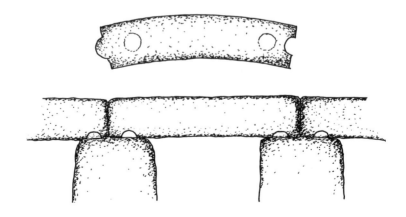

2000 BC - An idealised view from the southeast showing local tribesmen, and the broken-off half-width sarsen. From Stonehenge, by Edgar Barclay, London 1895.

1900 AD - Stonehenge viewed from the same angle as above, but before restoration in the early 20th century, showing a silhouetted bluestone (62).

1900 AD - View from the west, also before restoration, showing the once perilously leaning trilithon upright (56). Also visible are tenons on stones 56 and 60.

ROLLING STONES
the art of long distance megalith moving

The huge sarsen stones originated from Fyfield Down, near Avebury, and were dragged or rolled over 17 miles to Stonehenge. Some weigh in at 50 tons. Modern attempts to replicate this feat have shown how hard this must have been. The bluestones, weighing up to 5 tons, were no doubt easier, yet moving 80 of them over 150 miles from West Wales was no walk in the park either.

It is likely that the bluestones were hauled to Milford Haven, then rafted, either to the Bristol Avon, thence to Stonehenge, or around the Devon and Cornwall coastline to Hengistbury, a thriving prehistoric port on the Hampshire Avon (*opposite lower*).

The latitudes from which the bluestone and sarsen stones were taken are precisely one seventh of 364° and 360° respectively. These numbers formed the year in ancient calendars, for 13 and 12 month years respectively. Seven-fold geometry links the Aubrey Circle with the Sarsen Circle (*see page 179*).

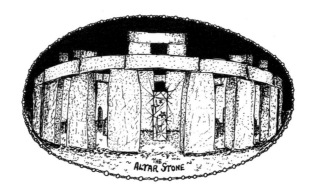

THE ALTAR STONE

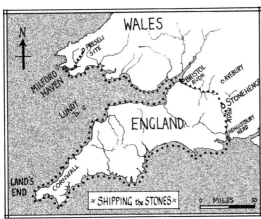

*Above: The 2000BC Ferriby
Boat, drawn by Edward
Wright. A reconstruction
has carried a bluestone.*

*Facing page: The Altar stone
is made of a sparkly green
micaceous sandstone found
adjacent to Milford Haven*

*Left: Two proposed land and
sea routes for the bluestones.*

ERECTING THE STONES
the fine art of levitating lintels

Fetching 50 ton sarsen stones from Fyfield Down and 4 or 5 ton bluestones from the Preseli mountains in Wales must have demanded a good working technology of ropes and levers, rollers and cradles. And plenty of spare time!

The large stones were dressed on site, and rolled or dragged to a waiting hole-socket. A crane-like structure was probably used to pull them up to the vertical. Perhaps the 'Y' and 'Z' holes (*see plans on pages 120 & 157*) held the props for this perilous process, for no stones were ever placed in them.

It is assumed, without any evidence, that the lintels were raised by progressively adding to the height of a wooden cradle whilst levering up the lintel. Presumably the lintel was then perilously slid across to meet the awaiting tenons in the sarsen uprights. Do not try this at home! Is it unfeasible to suppose that an earth or timber ramp may have been used? Levitation? Any other ideas?

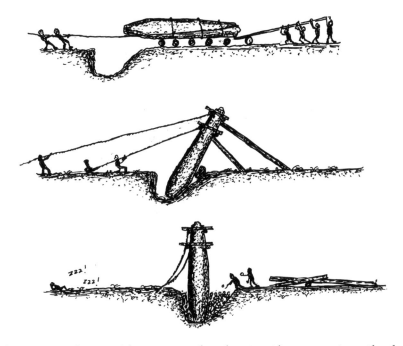

Above: Erecting the stones. The sarsens were dressed on site, with more attention paid to the inner faces than the outers. Holes were dug and the stones moved into position on rollers. After the sarsens were seated, ropes, props and levers were used to pull the stones vertical. Below: Lintels may been elevated by progressively raising the height of a wooden cradle.

The Modern Picture
our semi-ruinous legacy

The construction of Stonehenge began around 3150 BC and ended about 1500 BC. Thenceforth, it fell victim to the changing British climate and culture (*see graffiti of Mycean daggers below*). As late as 1917 the authorities submitted an application to demolish Stonehenge as "a dangerous hazard to low-flying aircraft"!

The relentless erosion of the sarsen stone by wind, rain and frost has produced some bizarre gnarling and pock-marks. In 1797 trilithon four fell, shaking the ground miles away. During the last night of the nineteenth century, a sarsen upright and its lintel fell (*stones 22 & 122 on the plan, page 147*). In 1958, these were re-erected and in 1959 several more stones straightened. In 1963, stone 23, which had been disturbed by the earlier restoration, fell and was quickly restored. Some fallen stones, over the ages, have disappeared off-site, perhaps to be broken up and used in less interesting buildings. The engraving (*opposite top*) shows the huge trilithon upright, stone 56, leaning perilously. Restoration work pulled it back to the vertical, but its mate still lies in pieces with its lintel.

· Stone 53 ·

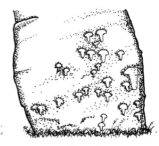

· Stone 4 ·

Above: Stonehenge in a thunder storm, 1829 engraving by Robert Wallis, after a 1827 painting by J M W Turner. Below: 19th century reimagining of Stonehenge.

THE GHOST IN THE MACHINE
reading the stones

So just what have we got here on Salisbury Plain? We know the site was prepared, surveyed, measured and marked out by people identical to ourselves, albeit very different in culture. Stones were transported, men and animals fed, equipment brought in and maintained. This was a colossal project of high importance to these people, and someone must have been the architect of the various phases, and known precisely what he or she was undertaking.

In 1963, Peter Newham discovered the geometry of the station stones at Stonehenge to be aligned closely with the horizon positions of both the extreme rises and sets of both the Sun and the Moon. Two years later this revelation was taken up in a bestselling book *Stonehenge Decoded*, by Boston professor of astronomy Gerald Hawkins. Despite being attacked by many archaeologists, it heralded the dawning of a new discipline, archaeoastronomy.

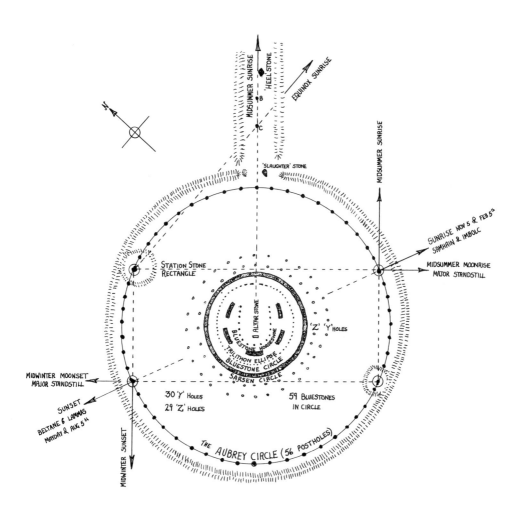

Above: In March 1963, Mr C A Newham wrote an article for the Yorkshire Post which revealed the solar and lunar alignments of the Station Stone rectangle. These alignments apply only around the latitude of Stonehenge—elsewhere the rectangle would become a parallelogram. The geometry is approximately octagonal (see page 179).

HERE COMES THE SUN
the longest and the shortest

At the latitude of Stonehenge, the annual range of sunrises and sunsets each sweep angles of forty degrees either side of an east-west line. The Bush Barrow lozenge (*see page 135*) displays these same angles. The midsummer sunrise viewed from outside the Sarsen Circle through the towering giant trilithon (*shown opposite*), appears from a point on the horizon along the avenue.

Although Stonehenge's axis was aligned to the midsummer sunrise during the Neolithic period, it no longer is today. A reduction in the Earth's axial tilt has caused the Sun to rise nearly a degree to the right since that time. However, because the heel stone flanks the right hand side of the Stonehenge axis (*see page 138–139*), the heel stone sunrise alignment (*below*) has become ever more convincing.

From the Stonehenge Avenue, the midwinter sun sets into the largest trilithon, nearly opposite the midsummer sunrise. In fact, as a processional walkway, the Avenue is far better suited to observe the midwinter sunset rather than the midsummer sunrise!

Left: Midsummer sunrise over the heel stone viewed from outside the Sarsen Circle, showing the trilithon framing the event. Note the off-centre alignment. The midsummer sun did not rise over the heel stone when Stonehenge was built, but to the left of it, directly down the Avenue. Picture from Edgar Barclay.

Below: The midwinter sunset occurs opposite the midsummer sunrise on a level horizon. It is known that a huge Neolithic midwinter gathering occurred in the Stonehenge area every year. Note that in this picture from Richard Colt Hoare's book of 1812 all the bluestones have been airbrushed out—no Welsh stones please, only ones from Wiltshire (compare p. 155).

WOODHENGE
another midsummer alignment

Nearly two miles north-east of Stonehenge is a field filled with 168 large concrete bollards inside an oval henge whose axes measure 140 by 130 feet. The bollards mark the original location of post holes that were once part of the substantial wooden monument from which Woodhenge takes its name. Some holes were six feet deep and some held posts that reached 25 feet into the air.

The site was identified from an aerial photograph in 1926 and soon excavated by Maud Cunningham. In 1958 its geometry was revealed by Alexander Thom as six concentric ellipsoids, with perimeters of 40, 60, 80, 100 and 140 megalithic yards, based on a 12:35:37 pythagorean triangle (*see opposite*).

Stonehenge and Woodhenge are contemporary. Both are aligned to the midsummer sunrise and both have their main entrance facing northeast. Both employ the megalithic yard. Stonehenge may have once sported a wooden structure and Woodhenge may have had bluestones placed in the huge holes in ring III. The present 'grey pillars' are a drab memorial to this neglected relative of Stonehenge, but at least display the original hole positions.

The centres of these two temples are spaced 10,033 feet apart, with an azimuth angle of 67.38 degrees, so form two corners of a 5:12:13 triangle, defining its '13' side. Interestingly, 10,033 feet is 13 × 2.722 × 283.53 feet, which relates it to both the megalithic yard of 2.722 feet and the mean Aubrey diameter of 283.6 feet.

Woodhenge has revealed its pedigree, as sister to Stonehenge.

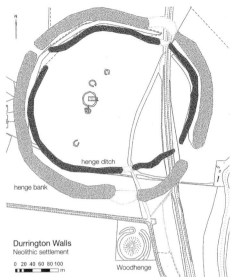

henge ditch

henge bank

Durrington Walls
Neolithic settlement

0 20 40 60 80 100
⊩⊩⊩⊩⊩⊏⊏⊏⊏⊏⊏ m

Woodhenge

Left: Durrington Walls, one of the largest villages in northern Europe, c.2500BC. Archaeological evidence has revealed that an annual midwinter feast was organised here, attended by people from all over Britain. Any midwinter's day party would surely have been considered incomplete unless it celebrated the sunset at Stonehenge (see page 159, lower). Survey from Ordnance Survey, 2007.

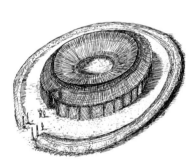

Above and right: Woodhenge, roofed or not, is an extraordinarily complicated piece of geometry. The larger postholes may once have housed stones. Based on a survey by Prof. Alexander Thom.

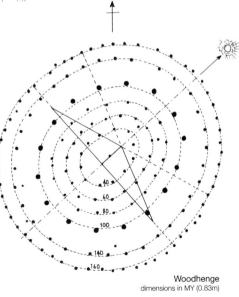

40
60
80
100
140
160

Woodhenge
dimensions in MY (0.83m)

CALENDAR CAPERS
the reasons for the seasons

At Stonehenge one repeatedly finds the numbers of the solar year and lunar month. On pages 15 and 157 we saw how at Stonehenge a 5:12 rectangle defines all eight solar festivals celebrated in our present culture. It also aligns with the extreme positions of the Moon.

The 56-hole Aubrey Circle suggests a calendar of 13 months of 28 days—a 364 day year (*opposite top*). The thirty giants of the Sarsen Circle suggest the Egyptian calendar of 12 months of 30 days— a year of 360 days. However, one of these uprights was deliberately made half-width (*stone 11 page 147, and top picture, page 149, the smaller stone fifth from the left*). Was this an attempt to represent in stone the 29½ day lunation cycle (the time between two full moons, 29.53 days)? The ancient Chinese were alternating months of 29 days and 30 days to produce the same 29.5 day average at around the same time. Twice 29½ makes 59, the number of 'Y' and 'Z' holes *and* the number of stones in the Bluestone Circle.

The bluestone horseshoe contained nineteen stones. Why? In nineteen years there are exactly 235 lunations—a near perfect repeat cycle of the Sun and Moon, known as the Metonic cycle. Other close repeat cycles occur after three, five, and eight years (*see next page*).

235 divided by 19 is 12⁷⁄₁₉, the number of lunations (full moons) in one year. Seven nineteenths is 0.368. The mean Sarsen Circle diameter is 3 x 12.368 MY (100.99 feet) and the ratio between the Aubrey Circle diameter and Sarsen Circle outer diameter is also seven nineteenths (*opposite*). Curious coincidences?

28-Day Calendar

THE SUN AND THE MOON

SOLAR YEAR = 365.242 days;   LUNAR MONTH = 29.531 days;
=> there are 12.368 moons per year = $12\frac{7}{19}$

1 Megalithic Yard = 2.72 feet =	
1 foot	1 Royal Egyptian Cubit (1.72 feet)

1 lunar month = 29.531 days =	
$\frac{7}{19}$ lunar months	$\frac{12}{19}$ lunar months

12 lunar months	Solar Year	13 lunar months
354.367 days	365.242 days	383.898 days

BANK   STATION STONE   SARSEN CIRCLE 104'   AUBREY CIRCLE 283'

THE 19-YEAR METONIC CYCLE
the marriage of Sun and Moon

After nineteen years, and within two hours of exactitude, the Sun and Moon return to the same places in the sky on the same date. This astonishingly accurate repeat cycle is named after Meton, a 4th century BC Greek astronomer. It does not involve the Moon's nodes and therefore does not produce eclipses. Another similar and important cycle takes 8 years, or 99 lunations and is synchronised with the 5 synods of Venus, the famous Venus pentagram; Avebury's outer ring once comprised 99 stones.

The 1st century BC historian Diodorus suggested that the Celts knew of the 19-year cycle. It si quite possible, for the Celts inherited the culture of the stone circle builders, and many fine circles, particularly in southwestern Britain, contain 19 stones (*Boscawen-un in Cornwall shown opposite*). The bluestone horseshoe at Stonehenge comprised 19 slender polished megaliths, brought from the Preseli mountains of west Wales, 135 miles as the crow flies. Some weighed over four tons!

There are 12.368 lunations (full moons) in one solar year (of 365.242 days = 18.618 x 19.618 days). The lunar year of 354.367 days (12 lunations) falls short of the solar year by just under 11 days, which after 19 years accrues to 7 lunations, totalling 12 x 19 plus 7, or 235 lunations. From these numbers, the *annual* number of lunations may be found: 235 ÷ 19 equals 12⁷⁄₁₉, or 12.368, the fraction better revealing the underpinning astronomy.

19 solar years is 6939.60 days; 235 lunations is 6939.69 days. So, the Metonic cycle may be written as 19 x 18.618 x 19.618 days.

CALENDAR REPEAT CYCLES

YEARS	LUNATIONS	ERROR	EXAMPLE
3	37	3 DAYS	
5	62	2 DAYS	COLIGNY CALENDAR
8	99	$1\frac{1}{2}$ DAYS	AVEBURY ISLAM
19	235	2 HOURS	STONEHENGE BOSCAWEN-UN MERRY MAIDENS

BOSCAWEN-UN

THE MOON'S NODES
the path of the moon crosses that of the sun

The orbit of the Moon is tilted with respect to that of the Earth by an angle of 5.14°. The effect of this difference between the planes of their two orbits is that the Moon travels very slightly *above* the ecliptic (the apparent path of the Sun around the zodiac) for about half the sidereal month, and then travels *beneath* it for the other half.

The two places where the Moon crosses the ecliptic each month are called the *lunar nodes* and they always lie opposite each other. The smaller illustrations opposite show these crossing points as observed from the Earth—but in truth, they are invisible!

Eclipses can only happen when a full or new moon occurs within 12½° or 18½° respectively of the lunar nodes, and total eclipses when the alignment is almost exact. These are the *eclipse limits* for lunar and solar eclipses.

The axis of the nodes moves *backwards* around the calendar, relative to the passage of the Sun and Moon, taking 18.618 years (6,800 days) to complete a circuit. The nodes thus move 19.618 days per year. To the ancients the nodes were thought of as the head and tail of a huge celestial dragon, *Caput Draconis* and *Cauda Draconis*, which swallowed the Moon or Sun during an eclipse, and the nodal period is still known as the Draconic year.

The Sun meets one node every 173.3 days (an eclipse season) and returns to the other after two of these periods have elapsed, this both defining and completing the *eclipse year* of 346.62 days.

Is it not the strangest thing that 346.62 = 18.618 x 18.618?

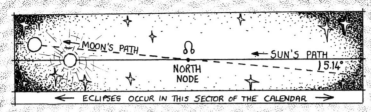

Above: Caput Draconis, the Dragon's Head or North Moon's Node,
where the path of the Sun crosses the path of the Moon in the Northern Sky.

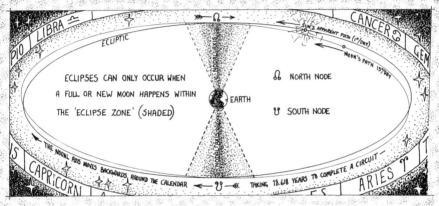

Above: Lunar and solar eclipses can only occur when the Sun and Moon are either
opposed or conjunct and close to one or other of the Moon's Nodes at the same time.

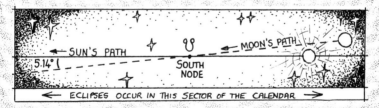

Above: Cauda Draconis, the Dragon's Tail or South Moon's Node,
where the path of the Sun crosses the path of the Moon in the Southern Sky.

THE BREATH OF THE MOON
major and minor standstills

The monthly extreme northerly and southerly risings and settings of the Moon gently 'breathe' in and out either side of the Sun's extreme solsticial positions, taking one nodal period of 18.6 years to complete the 'breath'. This greatly alters the possible maximum rise and set positions of the Moon each month with respect to the solsticial positions of the Sun. There are thus eight limiting 'lunstice' positions, four for rises and four for sets (*opposite top*).

The distance of these extreme positions of the lunstice from the solstice position is dependent on the latitude of a location. In southern Britain they occur more than 8° either side of the solstice positions (*opposite below*). In northern Britain, for example at Callanish (*see pages 312-213*), the swing increases to 17°. These extreme stations of the Sun and Moon drew the attention of Neolithic astronomers who made alignments of stones in their honour.

At the *major standstill*, the Moon describes her wildest monthly swings of rising and setting, gyrating to her highest and lowest ever paths across the sky, all within one sidereal month. Then, after 9.3 years, at the *minor standstill*, the Moon calms down and the range always lies inside the extreme solsticial positions.

In contrast to the Sun, Moon and planets, the backdrop of stars rises and sets with each star in its allotted position for scores of years, irrespective of the season or time of day. Over longer periods of time even these move slowly, stars-rising positions moving by about a degree over a human lifetime due to the precession of the equinoxes.

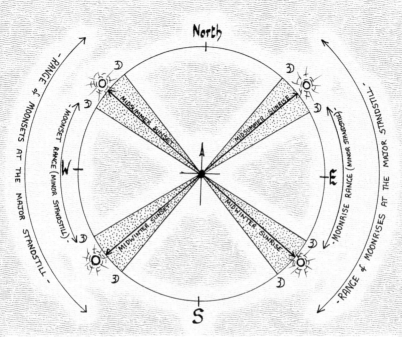

Every month the Moon copies the rising and setting dance that the Sun does in a year, also breathing inside and outside the solar positions over 18.618 years.

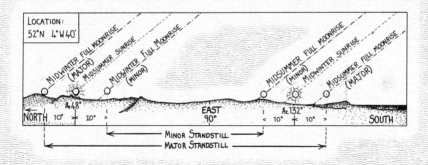

PREDICTING ECLIPSES
who nodes how holds power

Anyone who has tried to make a model of how the Sun and Moon move around the sky will end up, most simply, with a circle of 28 markers around a central earth. Moving a 'Moon-Pole' one position per day and a 'Sun-Pole' once every 13 days, both anticlockwise, replicates the motions of the two luminaries around the Zodiac, and this can provide an accurate calendar.

As we have seen (*pages 166-167*), twice every year, for about 34 days, a full or new moon will cross the Sun's apparent path in the sky (the ecliptic) to produce eclipses. These two eclipse seasons, which are 173 days apart, move backwards around the calendar, taking 18.6 years to complete a revolution.

The two places where the path of the the Moon crosses the path of the Sun are known as the *lunar nodes*, and by doubling the 28 markers to 56, as found in the Aubrey Circle (*shown opposite*), the 18.6 year period of the lunar nodes can also be incorporated. Conveniently, 18.6 x 3 is also almost 56, and eclipses may now be reliably predicted. Professor Sir Fred Hoyle was the first astronomer to comprehend this practical function for the 56 holes of the Aubrey Circle. A full or new moon within the shaded 'eclipse zone' predicts a lunar or solar eclipse. A lunar eclipse will always be visible at a given location if the Moon rises within the half hour before sunset.

Why not build one of these at home? Move the nodal markers clockwise three times a year, by one hole. The nodes will next coincide with the midsummer/midwinter axis in June 2020, and every 9 years and 110 days thereafter.

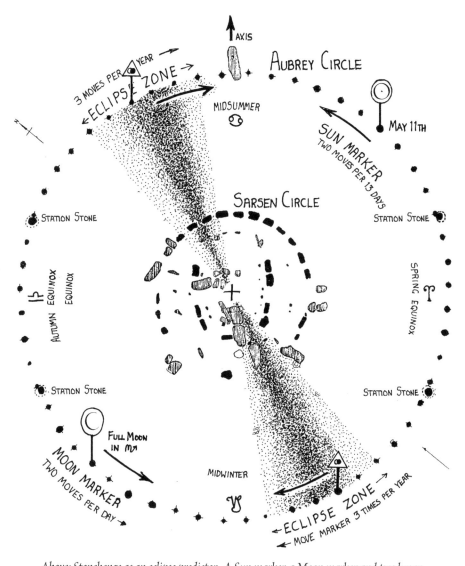

Above: Stonehenge as an eclipse predictor. A Sun marker, a Moon marker and two lunar nodes markers are all that are required to accurately predict solar and lunar eclipses.

STONEHENGE COMPLETE
not just a load of old lintels

Ever since the midsummer axis was first spotted by William Stukeley (*opposite*), it has been clear that there is an astronomical and geometrical component to Stonehenge. This clear alignment was first measured accurately by Sir Norman Lockyer in 1901, but the lunar astronomy was missed for a further half century because archaeologists had previously failed to recognise the importance of the Moon within megalithic culture.

As archaeologists Dr Euan MacKie and Lord Renfrew have proposed, an elite astronomer-priesthood seemingly able to extinguish a full moon or blacken out the Sun would have held enormous power over their tribe—eclipse predictors rule OK!

Many visitors think that the central stone constructions, the 'logo' of the monument, is all there is to Stonehenge, and hardly notice the concrete filled 56 Aubrey holes as they step over them. But, as Hoyle originally showed, these are numerically perfect for predicting eclipses, and can also show the Sun and Moon positions, lunar phase and the state of the sea-tides.

The Greeks, in the 4th century BC taught that the number 56 was connected with eclipses and dragons. The lunar nodes, which govern when eclipses occur, are still called *caput draconis* and *cauda draconis* (dragon's head and tail) in many astronomy books.

It would not affect the monument one jot to have the 'Stonehenge calendar' up and running today as an educational aid for visitors. Imagine the job description—but what long hours!

THE LUNATION TRIANGLE
integrating the Sun and Moon

One long-lost geometrical technique for integrating the crucial number of full moons in a solar year (12.368) is both simple and accurate, and Stonehenge fully supports its use in the Station Stone rectangle (*see page 142-143 & 157*). A 5:12 rectangle has a diagonal of 13. Any 5:12:13 Pythagorean triangle can generate a second hypotenuse to its 3:2 point with a length of 12.368 units (*one solar year, opposite top*).

The 153 fishes caught in the disciples' net in St John, Chapter 21, suggests arcane knowledge of the lunation triangle, for the square on the hypotenuse here is $12^2 + 3^2 = 12.369^2 = 153$.

The geodetic triangle shown opposite connects Stonehenge with the bluestone site, and is 2,500 times larger than the Station Stone rectangle. The right angle at Lundy Island corresponds well with the Old Welsh name for Lundy, *Ynys Elen*, 'the Island of the elbow'. In Welsh myth, the old straight tracks were under the protection of Elen, the goddess of sunset (the west). The Romano-British princess, Helen, who came from a western island, presumed to be Anglesey, was later said to have constructed long straight roads throughout the kingdom. Caldey Island, at the 3:2 point, hosted one of the earliest and prominent Celtic Monasteries, associated with St Illtud and St Samson (sixth century AD).

The three capital cities of mainland UK, Cardiff, London and Edinburgh also form an accurate 5:12:13 triangle, 2.5 times larger again. Finally, a great circle connecting the bluestone site to Stonehenge also passes through the Pyramid site in Egypt!

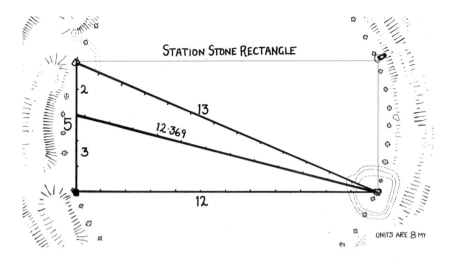

Above: *The 5-12-13 Pythagorean triangle at Stonehenge, showing the 5-side divided 2:3*

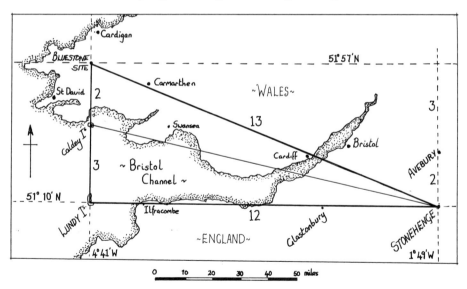

Above: *The 5-12-13 Station Stone triangle enlarged 2,500 times, showing Lundy and Caldey Islands at the corner and 2:3 point, and the Preseli bluestone site at the top left.*

RECORDS IN STONE
high spirits in the night sky

The phrase 'a length of time' may originally derive from an epoch when the length of a ruler, rope or set measure actually represented a time period—a technique manifested within many megalithic structures, which enshrine the time periods of the Sun and Moon.

For example, the Sarsen Circle's outer circumference measures 327.71 feet, while twelve lunar orbital periods last 327.86 days (99.95%). Here, one day represents one foot.

The Aubrey Circle defines the boundary of the Stonehenge temple, and has an outer diameter of around 3433 inches. The resulting circumference is then very close to 10785.82 inches, the product of the solar year and the lunar month, (365.24 × 29.53 days). Coincidence or deliberate design?

Meanwhile, a line drawn between Woodhenge and Stonehenge measures 10,033 feet, its angle defining the '13' side of an accurate 5:12:13 triangle (see page 175). Now, 10,033 feet is 13 × 2.722 × 283.53 feet, invoking the number thirteen, the megalithic yard (2.722 feet) and the mean diameter of the Aubrey Circle (99.98%). This same distance converted into remens (1.2 feet) becomes 8360.83 (remens), which is 8 × 2.722 × 383.897 days (thirteen lunar months) (99.99%). A forgotten science connecting space and time is revealed.

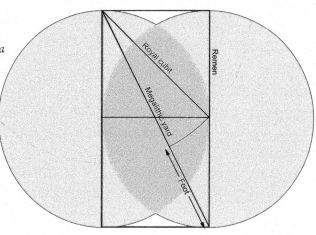

Right: Many megalithic units derive from the vesica piscis construction when the squares are given side lengths of one 'geographic' remen, or 1.2165 feet, 6/5ths of the 'geographic' foot of 1.01376 feet, used in navigation and cartography.

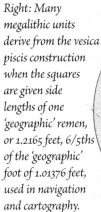

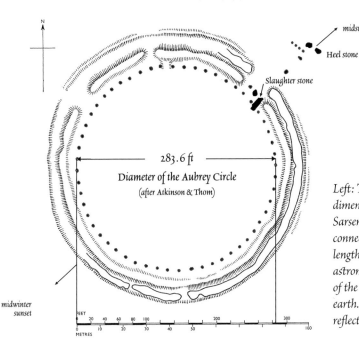

midsummer sunrise

Heel stone

Slaughter stone

283.6 ft
Diameter of the Aubrey Circle
(after Atkinson & Thom)

N

midwinter
sunset

Left: Through their dimensions, both the Sarsen and Aubrey circles connect familiar units of length with the principal astronomical rhythms of the Sun Moon and earth. Thereby Stonehenge reflects the dance of life.

FEET
20   40   60   80   100   200   300
0   10   20   30   40   50   100
METRES

SACRED GEOMETRY
how to build a temple

The geometry of Stonehenge uses the numbers seven and eight to produce the 7 x 8 = 56 Aubrey holes necessary for eclipse prediction (*see opposite*). John Martineau recently showed how the Aubrey Circle is precisely defined by an octagram suspended from the Heel Stone. The enclosing circle has the same radius as the long side of the Station Stone rectangle, 96 MY (261 feet). Furthermore, if every eighth Aubrey hole is marked out and connected as a heptagram, the shape correctly defines the mean diameter of the Sarsen Circle at 100.9 feet (= 37.1 Megalithic yards, or 3 x 12.368 MY, or 3 years).

Also, if the Aubrey Circle represents the earth, then the Station Stone rectangle emulates the tropics of Cancer and Capricorn.

The geometry of the sarsens and bluestones also beckons. Inigo Jones proposed a Roman hexagonal scheme in 1655. John Michell showed the Bluestone Circle 'squaring' the Sarsen Circle and connecting to the bluestone horseshoe by a hexagram, and John Martineau has proposed another octagram (*see diagrams below*).

 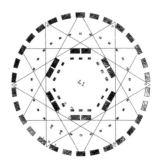

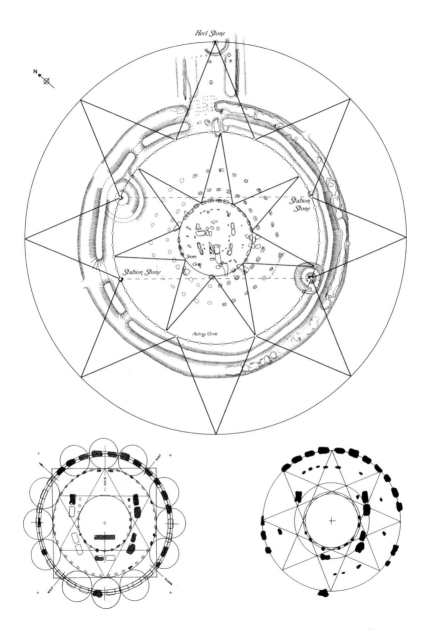

A Geodetic Marker

three centuries of enquiry

Geometry was applied not only within Stonehenge but used as a geodetic marker linked to other sites within a geodetic grid. A meridian line running due north from Stonehenge calls in on Arbor Low (*shown below right*) near Matlock, popularly known as 'the Stonehenge of the North', two degrees north of Stonehenge (99.5%). Further north the line passes within three miles of Druid's Temple near Masham, a bizarre folly of Stonehenge. Built around 1800 by William Danby and based on the inaccurate engraving in Camden's *Britannia* (*see page 127*), the present structure is located accurately three degrees north of Stonehenge. The meridian line then carries on northward until it cuts right through Holy Island on Lindisfarne, the site of a famous monastery, castle and a large bluestone outcrop! It then meets the Scottish coast at Peterhead *en route* to Fair Isle and finally Papa Stour, in Shetland.

Due west of Arbor Low is the famous passage grave, Bryn Celli Ddu on Anglesey (*shown below left, as it appeared in 4000 BC*). This forms an accurate 3:4:5 triangle with Stonehenge in units of 240/7 miles.

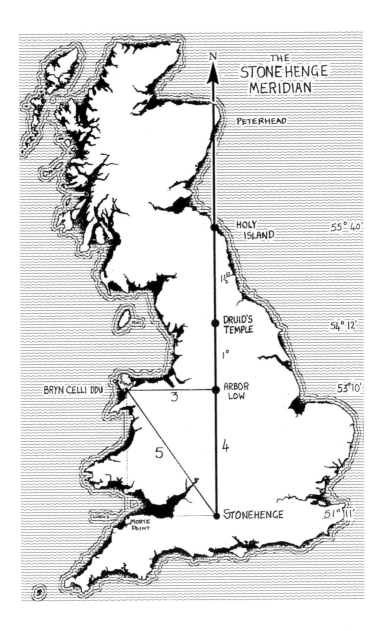

Sun, Moon & Earth

the revealed structure of the system

The diagram opposite frames a curious symmetry. Both the eclipse year (346.62 days) and thirteen full moons (383.89 days) are almost exactly equally spaced, at 18.6 days, either side of the solar year of 365.242 days. Because the eclipse year is the square of the lunar node period expressed in days (18.618^2), we can now state that the solar year is $(18.618 \times 18.618) + 18.618$, or 18.618 times 19.618. The number 18 added to $1/phi$, phi or phi^2 now delivers the following extraordinary formulae (to 99.99%):

$$18.618 \times 18.618 = 346.62 \text{ days (the Eclipse Year)}$$

$$18.618 \times 19.618 = 365.242 \text{ days (the Solar Year)}$$

$$18.618 \times 20.618 = 383.89 \text{ days (13 Lunations)}$$

The astronomy reveals the actual geometry and numerical structure of the Sun–Moon–Earth system (*opposite*).

In the diagram (*opposite*) imagine a solar eclipse at (1). The Sun then moves to meet up with the same node after an eclipse year (2), 346.62 days later. Passing the original eclipse point (1) at the end of one year, the Sun and Moon then meet for the thirteenth lunation at (3) (but without an eclipse).

An isosceles triangle, drawn to fit the angles generated by the astronomy, also then defines the solar eclipse limits, and has the remarkable property of replicating the numbers shown above as ratios. In addition, the shorter side has a length 12.368, the annual lunation rate. One marvels at this revelation of cosmic order!

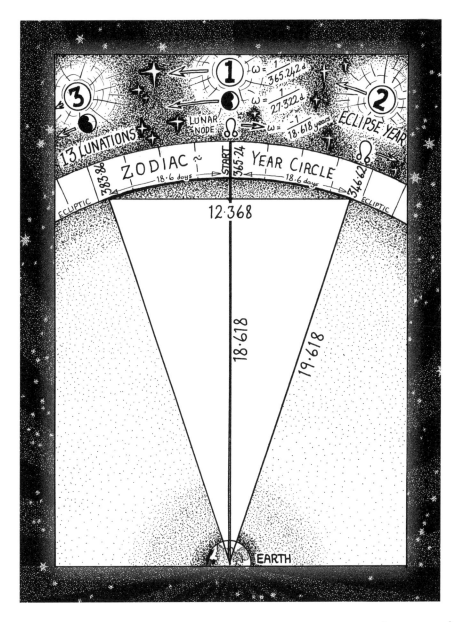

STONE AGE COMPUTERS
Neolithic cosmology revealed

In remote places in Britain survive many examples of curiously flattened stone 'circles', constructed some 4,500 years ago and named 'type-A' and 'type-B' by Professor Thom, the discoverer of the Megalithic yard (2.72 feet, 32.64 inches, 0.83 m).

Both type-A and type-B rings invoke a Christian symbol, the *vesica piscis*, the almond shape between two overlapping circles, here applied 2,500 years before Jesus. Stones are commonly placed intelligently to the geometry (*opposite*). Astonishingly, this design invokes the *same* triangle we have just witnessed underpinning the structure of the Sun, Moon, Earth system!

The right triangle has side ratios $1 : 3 : \sqrt{10}$. A hemp rope taken from the centre O to point P, and thence to B and A, has a length $3 + \sqrt{10} + 2$, which is 8.16227, exactly one quarter of the Megalithic yard, in inches. If length PB is considered to represent a lunation period, then the intersection of the vesica circle cuts it at 0.368 of its length (at X). If PB is now considered to represent the solar year, then PO represents the eclipse year, this ratio being either $\sqrt{10} : 3$ or 19.618 : 18.618. The ratios foot : Royal cubit : Megalithic yard may also be 'read' from this exquisite device.

This most beautiful analogue of the Sun, Moon and Earth system stores their key constants *and* the ancient metrology all within itself, as ratios. An awesome glimpse of an ancient wisdom is now finally revealed.

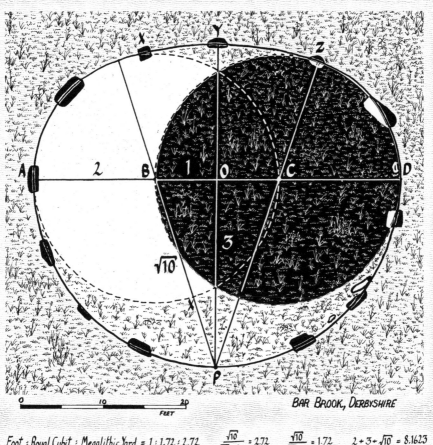

BAR BROOK, DERBYSHIRE

Foot : Royal Cubit : Megalithic Yard = 1 : 1.72 : 2.72 $\dfrac{\sqrt{10}}{\sqrt{10}-2} = 2.72$ $\dfrac{\sqrt{10}}{\sqrt{10}-5} = 1.72$ $2+3+\sqrt{10} = 8.1623$

The Royal Cubit is 1.72ft, 20.64"   The Megalithic Yard is 2.72ft, 32.64" $(4 \times 8.1623")$

Above: The exact same triangle as defined the marriage calendar of the Sun and the Moon on the previous page is mysteriously present at the heart of all of England's ancient flattened stone circles.

Inspirational Stonehenge
a source of wonder and amazement

Stonehenge may elude us, but it also inspires us. The monument taunts our smallness, yet celebrates our abilities. Our culture assumes superiority whilst those stones point to things we have forgotten, and they mock our hubris in so doing. As the poet Drayton wrote in 1612 in *Polyolbion*:

> *"Ill did those mighty men to trust thee with their story,*
> *Thou hast forgot their names, who raised thee for their glory."*

And to drive the point home, the American novelist Henry James wrote:

> *"There is something in Stonehenge almost reassuring, and if you are disposed to think that life is rather a superficial matter, and that we soon get to the bottom of things, the immemorial gray pillars may serve to remind you of the enormous backdrop of time."*

Many poets and writers have dipped their pens into the dark ink of James' 'immemorial gray pillars' and Stonehenge has also inspired many fine artists throughout history—Constable, Turner (*see page 155*), Blake and Henry Moore all worked with the monument, as did melodramatic lesser artists (*opposite*). Perhaps, like the black monolith in Arthur C. Clarke's *2001: A Space Odyssey*, Stonehenge enables a process of increased consciousness, most notably of the true rhythms of human life and the cycles of the Sun and Moon.

We moderns have lost most of that, and need with some urgency to reclaim our long-lost legacy from the past, here shown frozen in time and space at Stonehenge.

"It's true Edgar, the solstice was yesterday!"

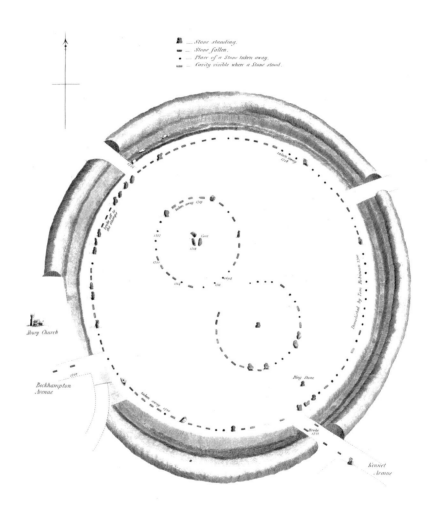

Abury Church

Beckhampton
Avenue

Cove

Ring Stone

Kennet
Avenue

Demolished by Tom Robinson 1700

AVEBURY

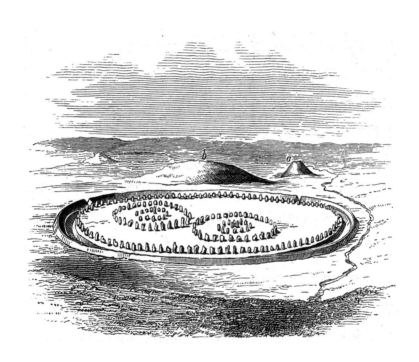

Evelyn Francis

Above: A plate from Stukeley's book Abury - A Temple of British Druids, *published in 1743, showing a view from the westerly edge of the of south inner circle looking south, and the great stones at the southern entrance where the avenue joins the outer circle.*

INTRODUCTION

Avebury is the largest stone circle in the world. Built between 3000 BC and 2500 BC it attracts around half a million visitors a year.

I have been visiting the great circles of Avebury since I was small, and in this pocket book I have selected the more prominent features of the ancient sacred landscape around Avebury—the stones, Silbury Hill, the Sanctuary, the Avenue, the barrows, the West Kennet Longbarrow, the Dolmen and Swallowhead Spring. Each of these need to be visited to really understand the site. The lost valleys, fairy dingles and witchy woods I will leave to the fleet of foot and keen of ear.

The diagrams used in these pages are mostly from William Stukeley's book of 1743; to my eye these better convey the beauty and grandeur of the place better than modern photographs.

Today, the Avebury circles have a busy road through their centre and constant traffic deafens visitors. The houses in the circle all carry electric circuits and by night televisions flicker inside this ancient place.

Avebury is a World Heritage Site, so I hope one day the road will be dug up and grassed over, and the circles once again will be granted the peace and dignity they deserve.

I am indebted to John Martineau for his kind assistance with the astronomy and geometry of Avebury, and to Robin Heath and John Michell for other important observations. Special thanks also to Steve Marshall and to Matt Tweed for their expert help.

I leave it to you, dear reader, to explore this extraordinary ancient temple, surely one of the foremost wonders of the ancient world.

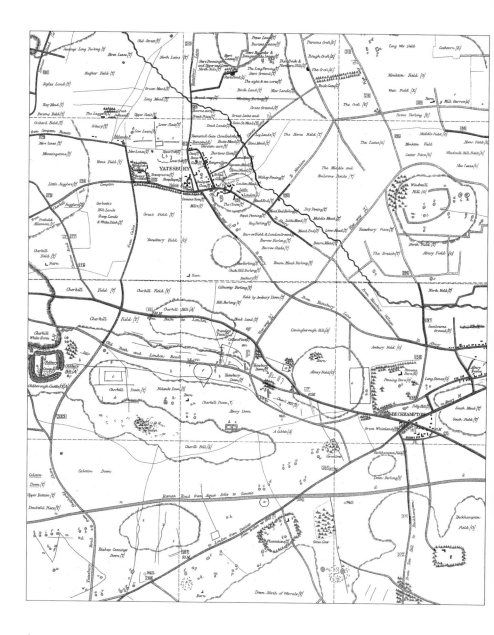

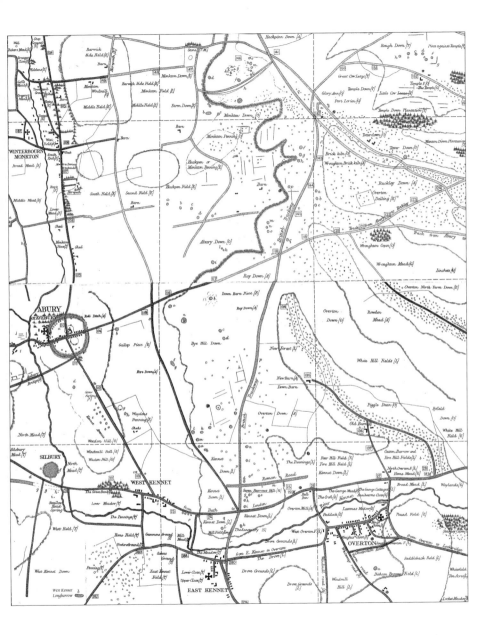

The

Temple downs

Hakpen

hill

Roy

Kennet avenue

Overton hill

spring

West Ke

Kennet river

Long barron

Wansdike

THE CENTRE OF THE ISLE
Avebury as the centre of the 'Michael' line

If you draw a line from the western tip of England to the eastern point then you will discover that Avebury is near the centre of that line. The line (known as the 'Michael line') is the May Day sunrise line and passes through many ancient sacred sites (*opposite top*). The line marks the sunrise for Beltane (May 7th) and Lammas (August 6th), and the sunset for Imbolc (February 5th) and Samhain (November 7th). These festivals lie halfway between the Solstices and the Equinoxes, the days of extremes and balancing. So if you watch the Mayday sunrise from Glastonbury Tor, it will rise over Avebury.

Avebury is also precisely at the centre of the three great watersheds of southern England. Water drains away from Avebury in every direction.

South of Avebury lies Silbury Hill, Swallowhead Spring and the West Kennet Longbarrow. Running northeast along the ridge of Hackpen Hill is the ancient Ridgeway track. The Ridgeway starts at the ancient springs and hollow yew tree at Alton Priors, then crosses another ancient earthwork, the Wansdyke, on top of the chalk downs near St. Anne's Hill, then passes the Sanctuary (close to the line of five barrows lower right in the picture opposite), before passing to the east of Avebury and heading off to the huge hillfort of Barbury Castle and beyond.

Walking east out of Avebury up the ancient track to the Ridgeway gives easy access to magical Fyfield Down, with its great sarsen stones and rare thistles. Just west of Avebury can be found two large stones, Adam and Eve, all that remain of a second avenue. To the north is the ancient 3500BC settlement of Windmill Hill. Huge barrows here may house the remains of the ancient kings and queens of Avebury.

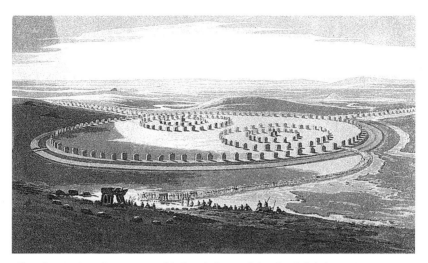

Above: Imaginative 19th century view of Avebury, looking south, based on Stukeley's engraving on previous page. Downhill from a gloomy dolmen in the foreground, a group of workmen rest on the side of the hill, admiring the view of the vast Neolithic temple, suddenly revealed by a shaft of sunlight, built by their noble ancestors. Silbury Hill can just be seen in the distance on the right.

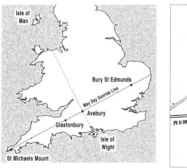

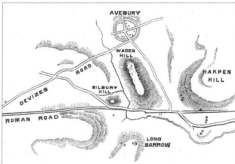

Left: Avebury lies at the centre of the island's westernmost-easternmost axis, also the May Day line, which passes through St. Michael's Mount and the Hurlers Stone Circles in Cornwall, plus the two longest abbeys ever built in the British Isles, at Glastonbury and Bury St. Edmunds. The ancient Ridgeway path, which runs northeast from Avebury, and the Icknield Way, home to Ivanhoe Beacon and the Gog Magog hills in the east, also form parts of the line. Right: Map of Avebury and surrounding area.

Stones from the Ice Age
getting to know the landscape

The Avebury complex is far greater than the stone circles themselves, and when visiting Avebury, it can be a very good idea to take time to wander widely in the area. A mile to the north lie the much more ancient barrows of Windmill Hill, and a few miles to the south lie the prominent earthworks around Adam's Grave. Exploring the area you may regularly stumble across a lost stone or a forgotten barrow (*opposite top*), and you will invariably experience changing views and perspectives which will all enrich your understanding of the vast and powerful sacred landscape in which the Avebury circles were sited.

For example, to obtain a glimpse of the landscape in more ancient times try visiting the small village of Lockeridge (*lower, opposite*), south of Avebury, where huge sarsen stones still lie where they fell when the ice melted twelve thousand years ago. And the enchanted valley and wildlife reservation of Fyfield Down to the east of Avebury is also well worth a visit for the same reason. It was from this primordial place that the large stones for both Avebury and Stonehenge were taken.

In fact, it could be argued that the best way to really get a feel for Avebury these days is to spend as little time there as possible, as the circles are badly affected by the lorries and electrical circuits of the houses which now pollute them. There are even public toilets right in the middle of this once central and sacred place—a bishop would surely not permit a toilet to be installed alongside his cathedral altar.

Viewing the henge from afar is therefore a must; it is good for the legs and can be very rewarding for the serious student of this most extraordinary of megalithic temples.

The Beckhampton Pot
evidence of fine craftmanship 5000 years ago

The pot shown opposite was found in one of the mighty barrows at Beckhampton to the west of Avebury in the nineteenth century and is illustrated in Richard Colt-Hoare's book. It is a fine example of what is known as flat-bottomed grooveware. Earlier pots found in the area date from the early Neolithic and mostly have rounded bottoms.

Later pots, such as the ones shown here, were often used as funerary urns, containing the ashes of cremated individuals. Many have been found in burial chambers and barrows around Avebury by generations of grave-robbers and archaeologists. Other examples are shown below.

Aubrey's Avebury
the first known sketch of the site

The first reference to Avebury appears in the 1610 edition of William Camden's *Britannia*, where he says:

> *"Within one mile of Silbury is Abury ... it is environed with a fair trench, and hath four gates, in two of which stand huge stones as jambs ..."*

Then, in 1663 Charles II overheard the antiquarian John Aubrey mentioning that Avebury:

> *"... does as much excell Stonehenge as a cathedral does a parish church".*

The King was fascinated and immediately set about visiting the stones with Aubrey. Aubrey's plan of Avebury is shown opposite, the earliest known. 80 years later, in 1743, William Stukeley produced the first book on the site. He thought it was built by people from Atlantis:

> *"When we contemplate the elegance of this country of Wiltshire, and the great works of antiquity therein, we may be persuaded that the two atlantic islands, and the islands of the blessed, which Plato and other ancient writers mention, were those in reality of Britain and Ireland. They who first took possession of this country thought it worthy of their care, and built those noble works therein, which have been the admiration of all ages."*

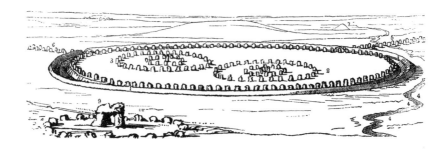

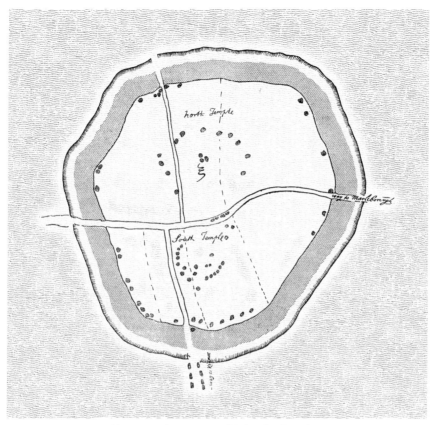

The seventeenth century map of Avebury by John Aubrey.

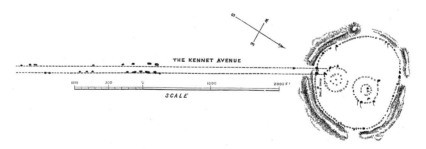

A Mighty Temple
the reimagined glories of the past

William Stukeley's famous 1743 engraving of the Avebury complex (*shown on pages 194-195*) showed a pair of avenues and multiple inner rings. It was an imaginative take on the ruined site that was later copied by numerous 19th century illustrators. The French engraving (*opposite*) is a good example, perpetuating the errors (*and see picture on page 197*).

Three stone circles survive today, one outer and two inner, along with the south-easterly avenue and the enigmatic man-made mountain of Silbury Hill, found south of the circles and henge. A short distance further south still can be found the impressive and partially restored West Kennet Longbarrow. To the east of Avebury lies the Neolithic Ridgeway track, which runs along Hackpen Hill in the far right of Stukeley's picture, passing the Sanctuary on Overton Hill at the end of the eastern Avenue. The Sanctuary had two stone circles in Stukeley's day.

The Avebury complex was interpreted by William Stukeley as a Serpent Temple with the Sanctuary as the serpent's head. Archaeologists have only recently rediscovered the westward avenue as they uncovered long-lost previously hidden stone-holes.

Flint tools from as early as 7000 BC have been found in the area around Avebury, but around 4000 BC people began living on Windmill Hill, to the north of Avebury, and started constructing long barrows soon after, followed by the cove at Avebury around 3000 BC. The outer circle and henge ditch, Silbury Hill and then the Avenue went up around 2500 BC. Some of the Avebury folk then went south, dragging the massive sarsen stones from Fyfield Down and Lockeridge, to create the huge trilithon uprights which still stand at Stonehenge today.

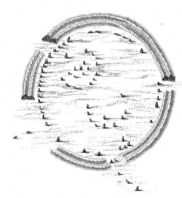

54. Plan en 1722.

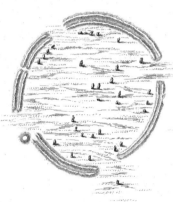

55. Plan dans l'état actuel.

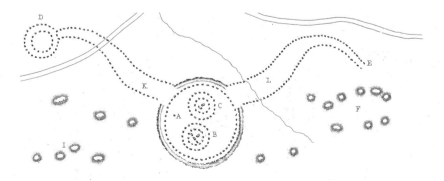

THE SOUTH CIRCLE
what was left of it in Stukeley's day

There are two stone circles at Avebury inside the outer 'Great' Circle. The section of the South Circle still standing today is shown (*opposite*), and has barely changed since Stukeley's times. The impressive entrance stones (two of which survive today) can be seen when approaching Avebury down the Avenue. As with the huge Stonehenge sarsens, the stones were carefully dressed on the faces pointing towards the centre of the circle, and left rougher on their outer faces. The South Circle originally consisted of 29 stones (*we explain why on page 218*), while at its centre stood a massive single stone, called the Obelisk (*see page 210*). Also shown is the strangely positioned *Ring Stone* whose stump may still be seen between the Outer Circle and the South Circle today.

There is evidence that the builders of Avebury attempted a third circle to the north of the other two but then gave up and dug the ditch instead.

THE SOUTH ENTRANCE
the approach from the Avenue

Avebury has four entrances, north, south, east and west, where the ditch is bridged and the henge has a gap.

Two of the largest surviving stones mark the entrance to the South Circle and as you approach down the Avenue, these giant guardians of Avebury's great Outer Circle hide from you until the last moment.

The left entrance stone, from outside the Circle, has a place to sit, and in a rainstorm will give you a shower from a hole above the seat. The gateway between the two entrance stones is thought to be very special as powerful 'ley' lines are said to cross there.

In Stukeley's day there were more stones than now. Avebury was being demolished as he watched and most of the stones we see today were put up in the 1930s by Alexander Keiller, the great restorer of Avebury, whose museum lies beside the church.

THE OBELISK
and the square in the South Circle

At the centre of the South Circle a huge stone, thought to weigh over 100 tons, used to tower over all the others at Avebury. Known as the Obelisk, it is shown fallen in Stukeley's picture (*opposite*). The twenty-nine stones of the South Circle originally surrounded the Obelisk. These were set at precisely the same average spacing as the outer circle, one every 36 feet, a considerable feat of surveying which shows the builders knew how to manipulate *pi*.

Twenty-nine plus the central one makes thirty, the same number of stones as the huge Sarsen Circle at Stonehenge, and, as we shall see, the number of stones in the North Circle too. The South Circle was 340 feet across.

To the west of the Obelisk (whose position is nowadays given by a large cross-shaped concrete marker), stand a row of small stones (*shown clearly on the survey on page 217*), which had been excavated by the restorer of Avebury, Alexander Keiller, in the 1930s. In 2017, new excavations led by Mark Gillings revealed these to be the west side of a 98ft square of standing stones, now thought to date back to 3000BC, making it one of the oldest structures on the site.

Huge obelisks are rare in the UK. However, across the Channel, in Brittany, they are quite common. For example, the Grand Menhir Brisé near Carnac was once the tallest prehistoric monolith in Europe. One purpose of the Grand Menhir seems to have been its use as a long range foresight for highly accurate observations of the Moon. Was the Obelisk perhaps used in the same way?

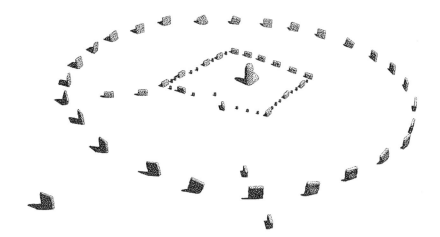

Above: The South Circle at Avebury, showing the huge Obelisk which used to stand at its centre, and the newly discovered square of stones which used to surround it. The Obelisk was later broken up by local farmers for building stone. Below: The Obelisk, as recorded by William Stukeley in his book of 1743. When standing, it would have been the largest stone at Avebury, visible from the top of Silbury Hill.

Part of the South Temple from the Central Obelisk 10 July 1723.

THE NORTH CIRCLE
gazing westwards

Of the North Circle just four stones remain today. Like the South Circle it is thought to have measured 340 feet across, although some sources reckon it nearer 320 feet. At its centre a 'Cove' (*see next page*) of three huge stones once stood, two of which remain today. There are still fallen

and buried stones at Avebury today, as Alexander Keiller's restoration was interrupted by the Second World War and never resumed.

It is thought that there used to be twenty-seven stones in the North Circle, with another three in the Cove, again making thirty in all. It was once thought that there may have been an inner circle too, of twelve stones, 170 feet across (*see page 205*). The fallen stone in the picture is still there, near the eastern entrance which is also nowadays the quietest and most attractive, the ancient route down from the Ridgeway.

THE COVE
a lunar clue at the centre of the north circle

Two massive stones still stand at the centre of the northern circle. Once there were three, in a cup-shape open to the north-east (the third one fell in 1713). The Cove points to the spot over Hackpen Hill where the most northerly full moon rises at midwinter.

THE GEOMETRY OF AVEBURY
Professor Thom's breakthrough

In the reconstructed survey shown opposite, you can clearly see the three stones of the Cove, pointing to the north-east (*illustrated on the previous page*). A cove at nearby Stanton Drew stone circles (*see page 260*) is similarly aligned to the northernmost moonrise; while another at Arbor Low stone circle in Derbyshire (*see page 31*) points to the southernmost moonset. Coves are thought to predate stone circles, with the Cove at Avebury being dated to around 3000 BC.

Professor Alexander Thom, the foremost surveyor of stone circles, published this solution for the strange shape of Avebury in his book *Megalithic Sites in Britain* in 1967.

Thom had discovered an ancient unit of measure, the megalithic yard of 2.72 feet, in many ancient stone circles, and Avebury further confirmed his theory. He noticed that the complex shape of the outer circle basically consists of seven separate curves and that four of these, labelled opposite as *a*, *b*, *c* and *d*, have the *same* radius, of 260 MY, while the two flat sections have radii three times greater, of 780 MY.

Especially interesting was his finding that three of the four centres of curvature lie in a precise 3-4-5 'Druids' triangle (*shown opposite*), here with sides 75, 100 and 125 MY. Professor Thom had discovered many other stone circles in the British Isles and France whose shapes depended on a 3-4-5 triangle, and was not surprised to find one at the heart of Avebury. Thom measured both inner circles both at 125 MY across (radius of 62.5 MY), with a distance of 145 MY between their centres.

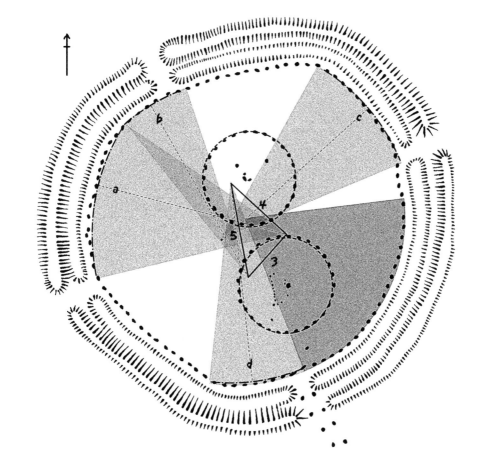

Above: Professor Thom's solution to the strange shape of Avebury. He discovered a Pythagorean 3-4-5 triangle with sides 75, 100 and 125 megalithic yards (of 2.72ft) lay at the heart of Avebury's geometry. Furthermore, four of the seven different sections of curvature have radius 260MY. Further geometry of the Avebury site is shown on page 221.

THE HEAVENLY SCIENCES
27, 29 and 99 stones

People often think of our ancestors as rough cavemen but they were also sophisticated astronomers. There are 99 stones in the outer circle at Avebury. Why 99?

Well, every eight years, Venus (our closest planet, and Goddess of love) draws an amazing fivefold flower shape round the Earth (*opposite below right*). But also, every eight years, there are exactly 99 full moons.

The numbers are: 2921.9 days for eight years, 2920 days for the Venus cycle and 2923.5 days for 99 full moons. So every eight years the Sun, Moon and Venus complete a full cycle. Perhaps the 99 stones of the outer circle each represent one moon of the flowery eight-year Venus cycle.

Islam is a religion which emphasises Sun, Moon and Venus—you often see Venus as a star beside a crescent moon on Islamic flags, symbolising the eight year cycle. And just to remind the faithful, there are also 99 names of Allah, each one a reflection, or a full moon, depending on how you think about it.

But what about 27 and 29 stones of the north and south circles? Well, for a start, the Moon takes 27.3 days to return to any given star, and there are 29.5 days between full moons! These are key lunar numbers. Also, 27 and 29 stones also add up to 56, the number of Aubrey holes at Stonehenge, and the secret number for eclipse prediction (*see page 170*).

The picture opposite shows Avebury's *precise* position one seventh of a circle up from the equator (if you take a GPS you will see the parallel actually goes through the centre of the Cove, as well as a peculiar relationship between Avebury and the Great Pyramid.

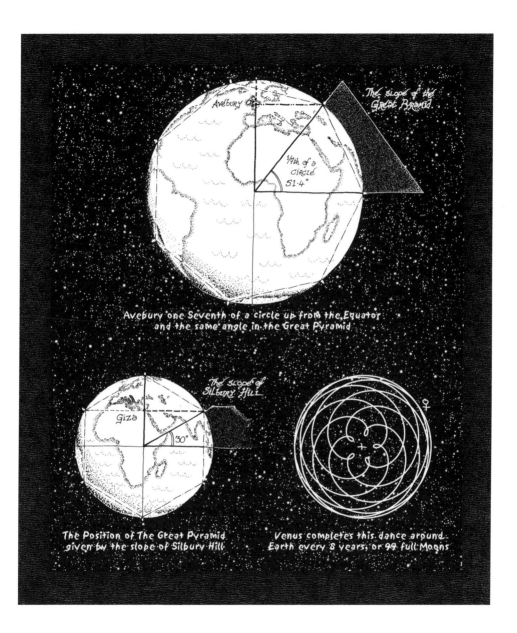

The slope of the Great Pyramid.

Avebury

1/7th of a CIRCLE 51.4°

Avebury one Seventh of a circle up from the Equator and the same angle in the Great Pyramid

The slope of SILBURY HILL

Giza

30°

The Position of The Great Pyramid given by the slope of Silbury Hill

Venus completes this dance around Earth every 8 years, or 99 full Moons

AVEBURY'S CORNERS
hidden angles & passages

Few stone circles are circular but Avebury is most unusual in that it has two sharp corners! Why? Well, the two tightest corners line up with the two centres of the inner circles to form two corridors.

The narrow corridor points exactly to the top of Silbury Hill and from the summit of Silbury Hill midsummer sunrise and sunset divide the horizon into two sevenths of a circle. The extreme winter points do the same, leaving a total solar horizon zone of three sevenths of a circle.

Now this is interesting, for if the inner radius of Avebury's inner circles is three, then the distance between their centres is seven. Three to seven. Avebury lies *exactly* three-sevenths of the way between the pole and the equator, the precise parallel passing through the Cove.

The angle between the wide corridor and the line connecting the two circles is again a seventh of a circle, 51° 25' 42", the exact latitude of Avebury on Earth. The sevenths continue to multiply.

A rectangle three wide and seven high gives a diagonal which is an excellent value for the tilt of the earth, currently 23.4°. And you may remember we saw on pages 216-7 how Avebury's outer circle is constructed from seven curves.

Seven was an important number to our ancestors as they knew seven heavenly bodies which moved through the zodiac, the Sun, Moon, Mercury, Venus, Mars, Jupiter and Saturn, and they knew of seven metals, gold, silver, mercury, copper, iron, tin and lead.

Like many examples of prehistoric surveying, one wonders how they did it.

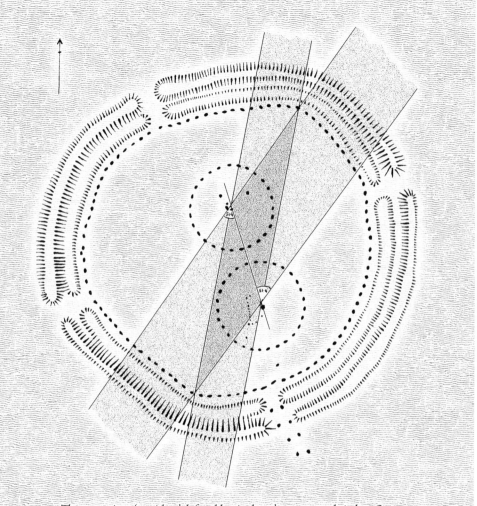

The mysterious 'corridors' defined by Avebury's corners and circles. One points to Silbury Hill, the other recreates the 51.4 ° angle.

THE AVENUE
a serpent of stone

The Stone Avenue at Avebury is very fine. It once connected the stone circles with the Sanctuary. Archaeologists believe the Avenue was built around 2500 BC, after the circles, and the ditch and bank had been finished. Finally, around 2100 BC, when they had finished the Avenue, the builders seem to have replaced the last of three huts at the Sanctuary with two concentric stone circles (*see page 224-227*).

The Avebury Avenue had about one hundred pairs of facing stones. Tall pillar-like stones (male) were chosen to face wider diamond or

Prospect of Kennet Avenue from

clover-leaf shaped ones (female). Research shows that people used to walk the outside of the Avenue.

Like much of Avebury the Avenue was restored in the late 1930s by Alexander Keiller. Stone rows are quite rare in the British Isles. The nearest to Avebury can be found at Stanton Drew, near Bristol. Merrivale in Dartmoor has lovely stone rows too.

The most extensive stone rows in the world can be found at Carnac in Brittany, France. Over 10,000 standing stones once stood in stone rows here, of which only 3,000 remain today. The French stone rows were erected between 3500 BC and 4500 BC, 1,500 years before the Avebury avenue.

the Druids tumulus on Hakpen hill. May 15.th 1724.

THE SANCTUARY
at the end of the Avenue

The Sanctuary lies at the end of the Avenue, beside the Ridgeway path. Marker posts today show different constructions from four different dates of building activity. Interestingly, the numbers of posts in each ring are mostly multiples of four (*see illustration on page 226*).

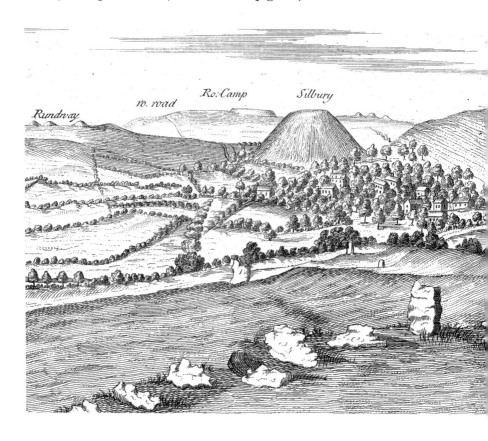

A timber structure first stood here 5,000 years ago, a few hundred years before Silbury Hill was started. A thousand years later, with Silbury, Avebury and the Avenue finished, two stone circles were built, either inside or replacing the 'hut'. The diameter of the outer stone circle (*shown below*) was 130 feet. Many stones still visible in Stukeley's engraving were removed soon after his visit. Just one remains today.

Windmill boll

Abury

THE SERPENT'S HEAD
and other ideas

William Stukeley imagined that, since the Sanctuary was found at the end of the Avenue, it naturally had to represent the head of a huge serpent. This idea is supported by writer Michael Dames, who adds that the Sanctuary probably represented the Candlemas point in a landscape fertility cycle.

Dowsers Hamish Miller and Paul Broadhurst found that the Sanctuary marks one of the crossing places of two enormous male and female earth energy currents which weave around the 'Michael line' (*see page 16-17*). Other authorities hold that the Sanctuary marks an arm of a huge pentagram set out in the landscape around Avebury, magically defining the positions of its elements.

It is thought that three successive buildings stood here, each larger than the previous, the final one containing the inner stone circle. It may just have been a display of decorated poles, and never covered. The large stone circle at nearby Stanton Drew has also been found to have rings of post-holes.

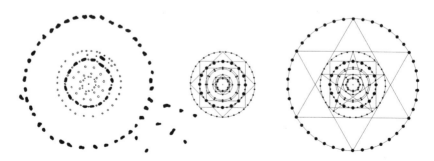

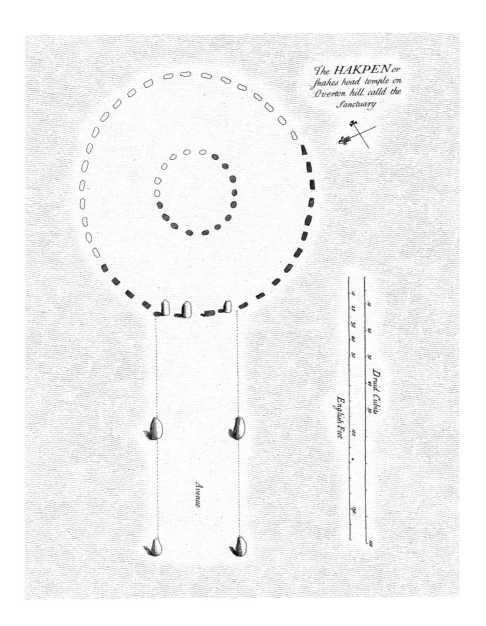

The *HAKPEN* or *snakes head temple on Overton hill. call'd the Sanctuary*

Druid Cubits

English Feet

Avenue

GLIMPSES OF ANOTHER AVENUE
the serpent's tail

There once was a second avenue leading west from Avebury. William Stukeley was convinced of it and imagined its route in his book of 1743 (*see page 194*). Stones were being taken away while he was writing and he shows the position of recently removed stones with a circle (*below*). Archaeologists now suspect that the second avenue terminated at Longstones Cove. Two stones remain today, Adam and Eve (*shown opposite*), part of a complex around the Longstone enclosure, with an adjacent longbarrow and another nearby at South Street dating as early as 3500BC, nearly a millennium before the circles were erected at Avebury.

Stukeley was fascinated with ancient wisdom traditions and founded the modern order of Druids to experiment further with his ideas of a long lost serpent religion.

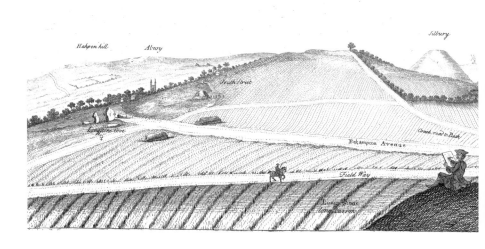

Above: Adam and Eve by the Longstones enclosure, three quarters of a mile southwest of Avebury. Adam (the near stone in the picture) was once part of the Longstones Cove, while Eve (the far stone in the picture) was once part of the Avenue. Below: Stukeley's engraving of the second avenue, which is now thought to have terminated at Longstones Cove, just visible to the left of the drawing.

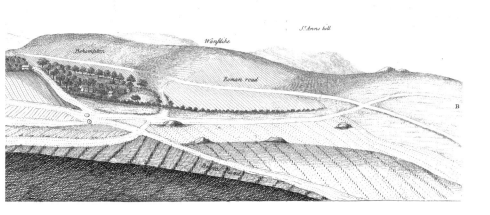

SILBURY HILL
the eighth wonder of the world

South of Avebury, over Waden Hill, Silbury Hill rises 130 feet from its boggy bed. The largest prehistoric man-made mound in Europe, built at the same time as the Egyptian pyramids, it is nestled into a bend in the River Kennet, just north of the Swallowhead Spring. The silky grass exterior hides a stepped conical pyramid built of seven concentric drums. Inside are many layers of chalk, mossy soil and gravel. Hazel twigs found at Silbury's core during excavations suggest it is five thousand years old. Like the henge around Avebury it is thought to have once been without its grass-covering—originally it would have appeared as a step pyramid of shining white chalk.

South of Silbury Hill is the central site of Swallowhead Spring, which flows from a small chalky tunnel. This is best visited on a frosty moonlit night in midwinter, when it can resemble something from a fairy tale.

Silbury

MERLIN'S MOUNT
a second pyramid

Silbury Hill is England's own Great Pyramid, built around 2400 BC, only a hundred years after the Egyptians had completed theirs at Giza. A second pyramid was also built a few miles to the east, and survives today as Merlin's Mount in the grounds of Marlborough College (*see opposite*). The ancient Britons built their temples in Megalithic yards (2.72 ft), and the Egyptians built theirs in Royal cubits (1.72 ft); the difference between the two is *exactly* one British foot.

The track shown in Stukeley's picture is still there today. A 19th century tunnel dug into the hill collapsed in the early 20th century, leaving a large hole in the top—English Heritage, guardians of the ancient monuments, decided to fill it up with polystyrene. The top of Silbury Hill is just visible from Avebury. If you jump in the air at the stone circles you can see the top of Silbury Hill over Waden Hill; if you lie down you can't. Saint Anne's Hill is behind Silbury Hill to the southwest. Later known as Tan Hill it has long been the site of a summer fair and travelling horse people still make their way there today. With a fire lit on Tan Hill, and dancers on Silbury Hill, mile-long shadows could be cast into the Avebury stone circles.

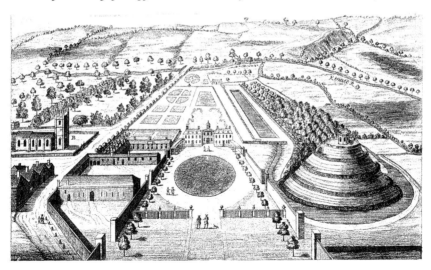

Above: Stukeley's diagram of Silbury Hill, suggesting a 40° slope. Other learned volumes suggest the angle is closer to 30°. Below: Silbury Hill's less famous sister, 'Merlin's Mount,' as drawn by Stukeley. Today the huge tree-covered mound still stands in the grounds of Marlborough College with a spiral path winding up it. Opposite: An iron horse bit, found in the hill in the 19th century.

HIDDEN CURRENTS
evidence of a lost science

In 1969 a book titled *The Pattern of the Past* was published. It was written by Guy Underwood, a Water Board dowser from Bradford-on-Avon, and published after his death. In the book he suggested that ancient peoples had been sensitive to subtle earth currents which he could detect using dowsing rods. Underwood had spent thousands of hours dowsing ancient sites across the country, even comparing surveys executed at different phases of the Moon. He proposed that stone circles, burial mounds and later churches built on top of more ancient sites were all positioned at places where these telluric currents converged.

Underwood's picture (*opposite top*) shows a map of the subtle lines of force at the beginning of the Avebury Avenue, where it connects with the southern stone circles. The second image (*opposite bottom*) shows his geodetic survey of Silbury Hill, complete with subtle energy lines, which he called 'aquastats'. In a very strange way the diagram captures something about the potent feeling of the place. Anyone visiting the site will agree that there is a distinct quality to being there which these pictures capture. Were our ancestors engineering the energy? There is so much we still do not understand.

Dowsers are still used today by water authorities, builders, farmers and telephone companies to find water, pipes and cables. Archaeologists also sometimes use them to locate hidden or buried walls. Yet this ancient art remains unexplained, even secretive, and few practitioners will openly admit to using it in the current climate. Many dowsers believe that the art may once have been more widespread and natural, possibly forming part of an ancient science and perception, now almost lost.

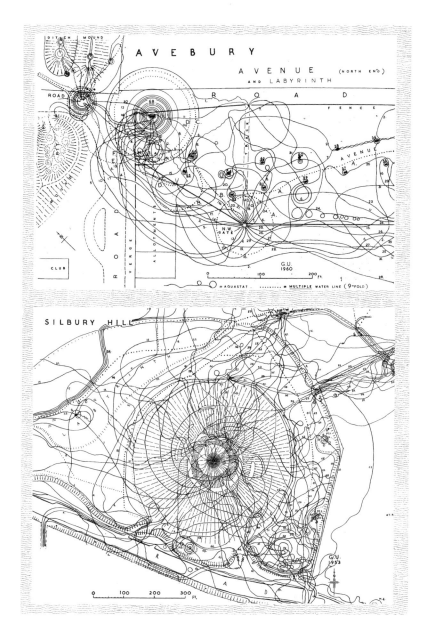

West Kennet
the longbarrow

LONGBARROWS AND DOLMENS
the Avebury quoit

The previous page shows Stukeley's engraving of the West Kennet Longbarrow. Built around 3650 BC, nowadays it has been opened up and you can go inside and poke around in the ancient chambers in the east end (*survey below*). No one really knows what longbarrows were built for. Professor John North recently found that many of them are precisely aligned on the rising of bright stars, something the Egyptian Pyramids do as well. Longbarrows appear 1000 years earlier than stone circles, and are often found on the edge of chalk deposits, beside cursuses. Cursuses are yet another megalithic mystery—huge mile-long runway-like things built all over the country for no known reason.

Some people think long barrows were kingly burial chambers, because bones are often found inside in small chambers off the main passageway, others think that they were early churches of some kind. They could have been both—we still bury our kings in churches.

On the other side of Fyfield Down is a dolmen, close to the A4. Known as the *Devil's Den*, it consists of a capstone suspended on three uprights. Dolmens like this one were often covered with an earthen mound. It is not known if they were burial places, meditation chambers or Neolithic follies. Another peculiar piece of the Neolithic puzzle!

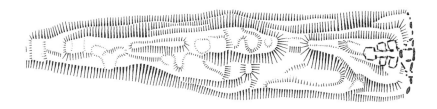

Above: The Devil's Den dolmen, at the bottom of Fyfield Down, today most easily accessed from the A4 at Clatford. Many ancient sites were given the D-name. The countryside is full of Devil's Stones - Devil's Dykes, Devil's Chairs and Devil's Punchbowls abound. This probably all goes back to Bacchus, and the shaggy legs and goaty horns of Pan, god of the wild, and friend of the faeries. Many places (and people) with strong connections to the ancient earth traditions suffered as sensitive understanding of nature was replaced by a fear of the unknown. Pan was turned into a evil devil, the image of Lucifer, who was previously the setting morning star, Venus. Despite centuries of repression, different levels of tradition nevertheless clung on in various remote parts of the British Isles, as they do elsewhere in the world.

MYSTERIOUS MOUNDS
barrows everywhere

Round barrows litter the ancient landscape around Avebury. There are various kinds—Bowl Barrows, Bell Barrows, Disc Barrows, Pond Barrows, Saucer Barrows, Bea Barrows and many others. Along the Ridgeway they are found clustered together in groups and today boast glorious stands of beech trees, planted as a fad in Victorian times.

Barrows sometimes have skeletons in them; sometimes they contain a

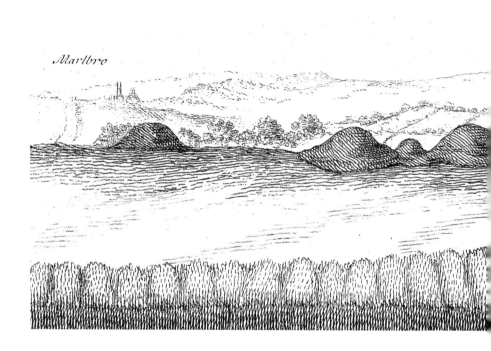

Marlbro

circle of stones. On rare occasions they contain buried treasure, and this has led to many a fruitless and destructive excavation over the centuries.

Some people think barrows represent constellations of stars, mapped down onto the earth, others have suggested they are built where early crop circles appeared (some crop circles look very like Neolithic rock carvings) or even where spaceships landed long long ago. In later times great warriors may have been buried in barrows, but many of the earlier ones are empty. Wilhelm Reich thought they were part of the earth-energy grid, functioning a little like electrical condensers.

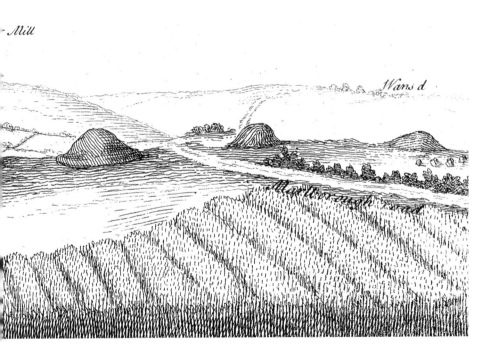

MORE MYSTERIES
lost artifacts and patterns of unicorns

So much has been lost. The dolmen (*opposite top*) and the magical barrow (*below*) were both recorded by Stukeley in his book on Avebury. Both are no longer with us. Stukeley wrote of the Monkton Millbarrow:

> *"In Monkton, west of the town, is a large and flat long barrow … 215f long 55 broad set round with great stones. It stands due east and west, the broadest end eastward. Its breadth the fourth part of its length: a most magnificent sepulchre, and call'd Milbarrow."*

Far away to the northeast on the Ridgeway path can be found the ancient Uffington White Horse hill figure, and another little Silbury Hill called Dragon Hill. Many other more modern White Horses cluster in the area and if you draw lines between them they cross at Avebury.

Abury

Above: *Ruined dolmen, now destroyed. near Winterbourne Monkton, north of Avebury. Below: The Millbarrow at Winterbourne Monkton, little trace of which survives today. Rediscovered in 1987, it was excavated in 1989, revealing a chambered tomb dating to c.3200 BC with facade and eastern chamber.*

THE FUNCTION OF AVEBURY
Sun, Moon and Venus

The world's oldest stone circles are at Göbekli Tepe, on the Turkish-Syrian border (*below*). Built between 9000 BC and 7500 BC, they were aligned to the rising of Orion, with new ones being built every 500 years when this alignment no longer held true, a perfect way to study the 25,800-year precessional cycle. Maes Howe, in the Orkney Islands, is a chambered tomb aligned for the full swing of midwinter sunrises, rather than the midwinter sunrise at the time it was built, a perfect way to study the 41,000-year obliquity cycle. The ancient Maya discovered that these two long cycles relate as 5:8 of their 5125-year Suns. At Carnac in Brittany, France, a simple geometry connects the swing of the Sun and the Moon. Everywhere we look, the ancients were interested in connecting Heaven and Earth, and understanding both. Avebury is no exception.

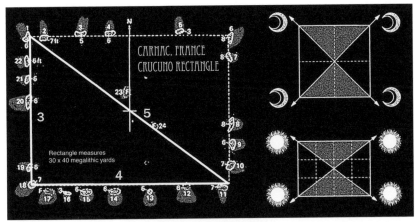

Diagrams: Howard Crowhurst

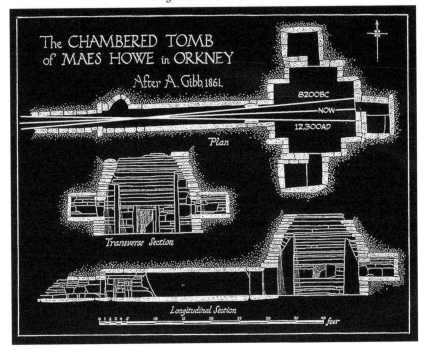

An early depiction of a druidical grotto. Here the Welsh druids are hiding Caractacus who is meeting some English soldiers, from Munimenta Antiqua by E. King, 1799.

STANTON DREW

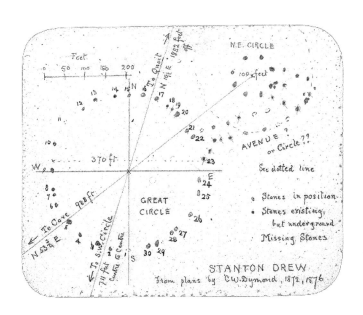

Gordon Strong

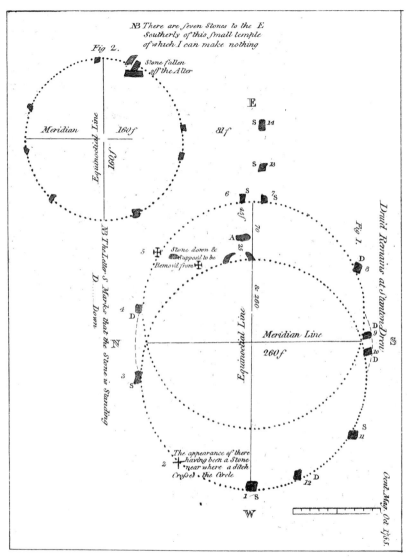

A fanciful geometrical interpretation of Stanton Drew from the Gentleman's Magazine of 1785.

INTRODUCTION

Stone circles are found throughout Great Britain and Europe, but only Avebury and Stonehenge top the magnificence of the triple stone circles of Stanton Drew in Somerset. Although little is known of this third great temple of southern England, it is true to say that modern techniques are at last beginning to unravel its ancient secrets. A 1997 English Heritage geophysical survey revealed that the stone circles are the remains of a far more elaborate site than was previously believed, with similar features to Woodhenge and the Sanctuary near Avebury.

As with other Neolithic sites, the accurate astroarchaeological alignments of the Sun and Moon cycles suggest that the so-called 'savages' who built these magnificent monuments were much smarter than current preconceptions allow. At the same time, they remind us how the circles would have played an integral part in ancient social and religious life. Questions surrounding these issues and others, such as quite how such mighty stones were quarried, transported, positioned and erected, still baffle the modern engineer and remain some of the most elusive mysteries surrounding our ancient cousins.

What we do know is that the construction of stone monuments began around 3500 BC and continued for over 2,000 years, marking a period when our forebears began more and more to settle, and thus to begin to erect more permanent structures. The virtually untouched megaliths of Stanton Drew might thus be viewed as a gateway to the lost knowledge of our West Country ancestors.

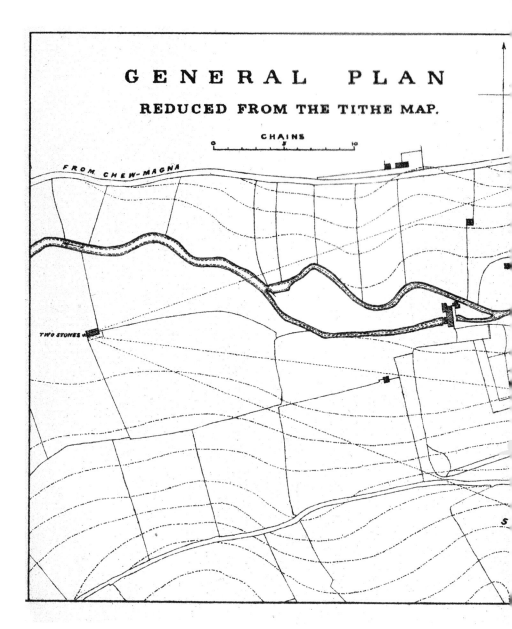

GENERAL PLAN
REDUCED FROM THE TITHE MAP.

CHAINS

FROM CHEW-MAGNA

TWO STONES

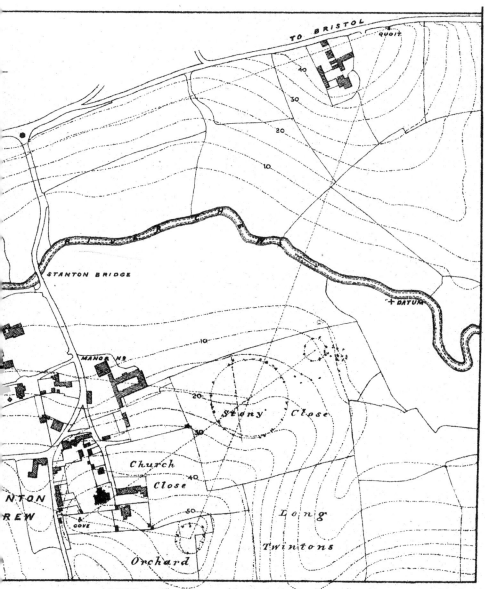

C. W. Dymond's 1896 survey of the site, clearly showing two westerly stones, now vanished.

EARLY PLANS
antiquarian maps and surveys

The circles at Stanton Drew were first noted by the 17th century antiquarian, John Aubrey, in a sketch of 1664 (*opposite top*). At about the same time, a Mr. John Wood visited Stanton Drew and made a plan of the site, but his visit was accompanied by a storm and the villagers accused him of having 'Disturbed the Guardian Spirit of the metamorphosed stones'. Sir William Musgrove next surveyed the site in 1716.

In 1723, the first comprehensive drawings of the stones were made by William Stukeley (*next page*), who believed the site comprised part of a sacred pattern with centres at Stonehenge and Avebury.

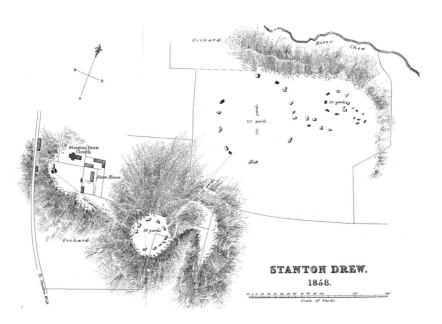

STANTON DREW.
1858.

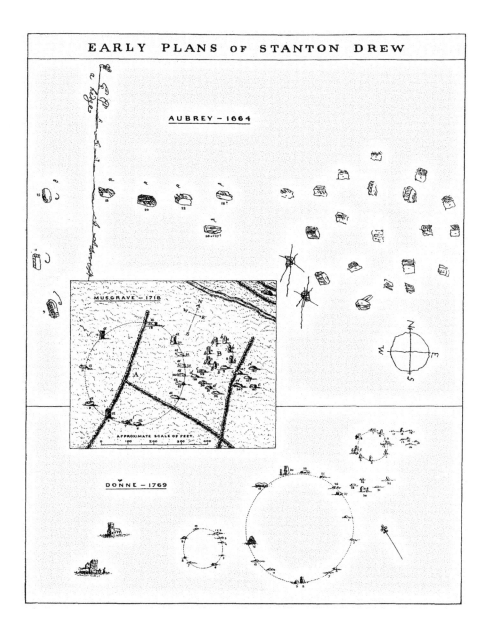

EARLY PLANS of STANTON DREW

AUBREY – 1664

MUSGRAVE – 1718

APPROXIMATE SCALE OF FEET.

DONNE – 1769

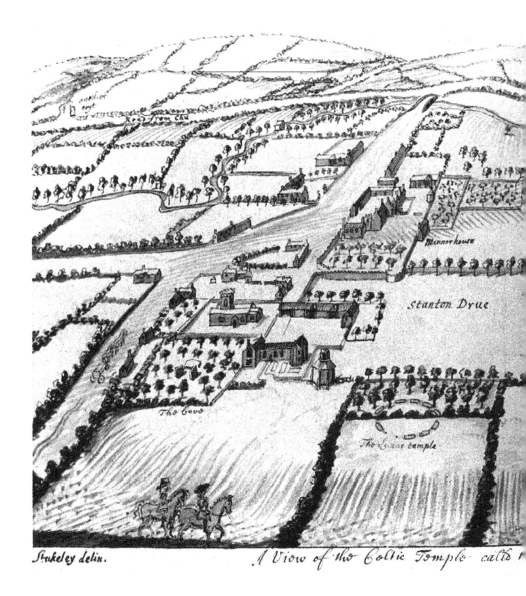

anolher
pot

Road from Chu

Mannerhouse

stanton Drue

The Cove

The great temple

Stukeley delin.

A View of the Celtic Temple call'd t

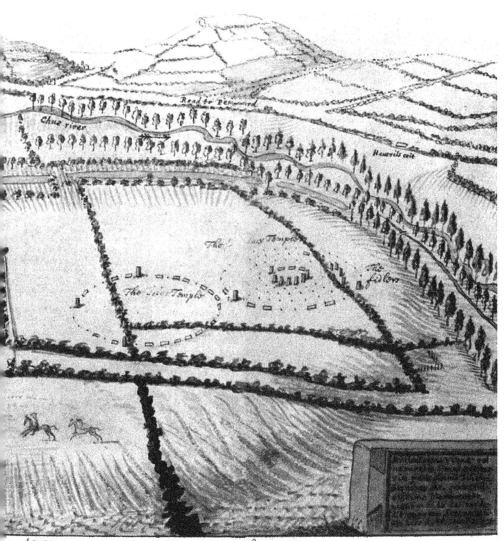

Chu river

Read to Pensford

Hauevils croit

The ... Temple

The Sun Temple

The fidlers

Weddings at Stanton Drue by 1723.

AN OVERVIEW OF THE SITE
the megalithic complex

Stanton Drew consists of three stone circles, erected around 2500 BC. The most prominent, known as the Great Circle, once had 30 stones (like Stonehenge) of which 27 survive today. With a diameter of approx 113 m (371 ft) and an area of some 10,000 square metres (108,000 sq ft), making it second in size only to Avebury. Like its sister temple in Wiltshire, it

was also originally approached by an avenue of standing stones.

The two other circles are situated to the northeast and southwest respectively. The Northeast Circle is almost intact with 8 large stones surviving today, and measures 29.6m (97ft) in diameter. The Southwest Circle measures 43m (141ft) across and has 12 smaller stones.

An avenue extends from the northeast of the Great Circle towards the nearby River Chew, while a second avenue once connected with it from the Northeast Circle (*see diagram on following page*).

A GREAT HENGE
surrounding the site

We now know that an enormous henge ditch, 135m in diameter and 7m wide, once encompassed the main circle at Stanton Drew with an opening to the north-east, perhaps allowing sight of the midsummer sunrise. During excavations several pits were also found, five in the central area of the rings and four in the Northeast Circle, in a quadrilateral pattern aligning with opposing pairs of the eight stones of that circle. The pits may have contained posts or stones which were removed, possibly an earlier smaller version of the present monument.

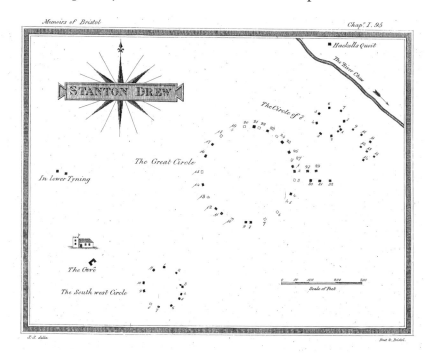

Above left: Hauteville's Quoit, in a 19th century woodcut by William Barnes, named after 13th century crusader Sir John Hauteville. Today what's left of the construction lies fallen near the Hauteville Quoit Farm. It may once have formed a dolmen, similar to Lanyon Quoit, Penzance, Cornwall, illustrated above right. Below: Lithographs by Charles Hullmandel [1789-1850] of Stanton Drew. The lower image on the left shows the Cove.

THE COVE
a sister to Avebury

The Cove (derived from Old English *cofa*, an alcove, and from the ancient German for hollow place) is today situated in the garden of the Druids Arms public house, a short distance from the main site.

Consisting of two still-standing stones with one recumbent slab separating them, all three of varying sizes, the three stones of the Cove are mineralogically diverse from the stones comprising the stone circles, and are thought to have been erected much earlier, around 3500 BC. The stones of the cove also stand on top of an even earlier long barrow burial chamber.

The Stanton Drew cove, similar to the one at Avebury, points to the position of northernmost moonrise.

The "Cove", Stanton Drew — looking E.

H.M.J.U.

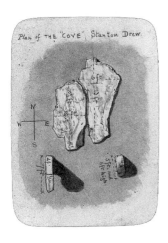

Facing page and above left: *Two measured drawings of the Stanton Drew cove by painter Henry Michael John Underhill [1855-1920]. Above right: The stones of the Cove as they appeared in the 19th century, hidden in an orchard. Below the Cove as it appeared in William Stukeley's* Itinerarium Curiosum *of 1776 (based on a drawing by Stukeley made in 1723).*

WOODEN POSTHOLES
building, ritual forest or raised platform

Possibly contemporary with the henge ditch enclosure, and on the site of what would later become the Great Circle, once stood a forest of wooden posts, larger and older than the examples at either Avebury or Woodhenge. When originally constructed, four to five hundred oak pillars, probably a metre (3.28 ft) in diameter and 26 feet in height, and each weighing 5 tons, occupied an area about the size of a football field. They were set in nine concentric circles, a highly symbolic number (there are nine worlds in many ancient cosmologies), and would likely have been carved or decorated.

This sophisticated structure was discovered in 1997 by the English Heritage geophysical survey and could easily have accommodated a thousand people if not more, suggesting its use as a possible focal point for social or religious gatherings. A common theory is that the site might have been dedicated to funerary ritual, but a host of other explanations have been put forward.

Britain boasts many other woodhenge sites (or timber temples, as some authorities quaintly refer to them), including Balfarg in Fife, Scotland and Mount Pleasant in Dorset and the Seahenge site on the Norfolk coast, but Stanton Drew is the largest of them all.

The woodhenge was eventually replaced by the stones of the Great Circle, a similar story to the Sanctuary at Avebury, where a stone circle still stood in Stukeley's day replacing the original roundhouse there. Whether the stones formed part of the original woodhenge design or came later still remains to be established.

Above: Visualisation of Stanton Drew by Michael Bott and Rupert Soskin. The posts are too close together to usefully form a roundhouse or structure like the Sanctuary at Avebury, or Woodhenge, near Stonehenge. Was it in fact a ritual forest for a boar- or deer-hunting game? Or were the posts put in place to support a platform or series of walkways for some other game or spectacle? Below: Large open-centred roundhouse, courtesy Historic England.

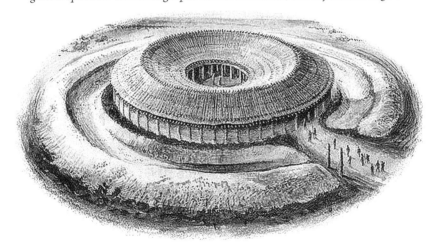

ALIGNMENTS
ley-hunting at Stanton Drew

Ley-lines (alignments of ancient sites over distance) appear to be evident around Stanton Drew. A line running from the Cove, for example, passes through St. Mary's church, on to the Great Circle and to the centre of the Northeast Circle.

A longer ley line runs from the church to the Iron Age fort at Dolebury Camp and then on to Brean Down. Yet another is said to pass through the stones at the ancient settlement at Cameley (linked with the Knights Templar and the Holy Grail) on its way to Maes Knoll and subsequently to the Market Cross in the old city centre of Bristol. Dundry Down and Cadbury Camp (at Tickenham) are also thought to be aligned with Stanton Drew.

Importantly, from the centre of the Great Circle the midsummer sunrise in 2,000 BC would have been at the point where Hauteville's Quoit is located, on an alignment that passes through the exact centre of the Great Circle to the centre of the SW Circle (*opposite top*).

On a flat plain midsummer sunrise will exactly oppose midwinter sunset, but at Stanton Drew, due to the lie of the land, the midwinter sunset in 2,000 BC from the centre of the Great Circle would have aligned with the Cove, on a line back through the centre of the Great Circle to the NE Circle. This midwinter line is at a bearing which suggests a hidden pentagonal geometry as it is defined by a pentagram pointing due east (the traditional geomantic orientation of a pentagram or pentagon in the landscape). The midsummer line is similarly defined as five-ninths of the way round from north.

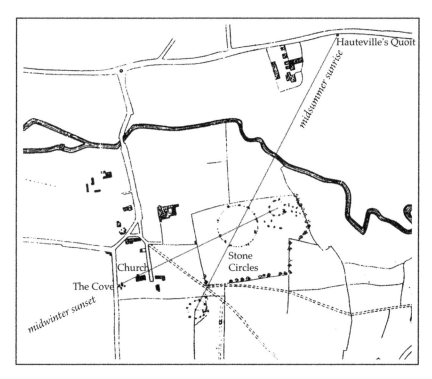

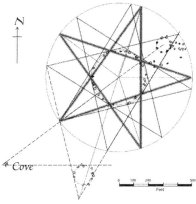

Above: Schematic diagram by C. W. Dymond, showing midsummer sunrise and midwinter sunset alignments as defined by the geometry of the primary elements at Stanton Drew.

Left: Diagram by J. Martineau showing the 144-degree pentagonal angle created by the midwinter sunset line.

GEOMETRY OF THE CIRCLES
triangles & octagons

It was C. W. Dymond, in his 1877 essay *Megalithic Monuments at Stanton Drew*, who first noticed the edge alignment between the three circles of the monument (*shown as a dotted line in the diagram lower opposite*). Little did he realise at the time what he had stumbled upon, for it was not until the 20th century, with Alfred Watkins' perception that edge-alignments are common in Neolithic alignments, and the astroarchaeological discovery that the edge alignment at Stanton Drew also marks the southernmost moonset from the site, that the full importance of this piece of the jigsaw began to be appreciated. Another important relationship present at Stanton Drew is a northerly edge-alignment (*shown as a dotted line opposite top*), almost identical to the layout of the Avebury henge relative to the position of Silbury Hill.

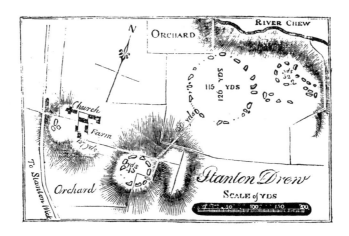

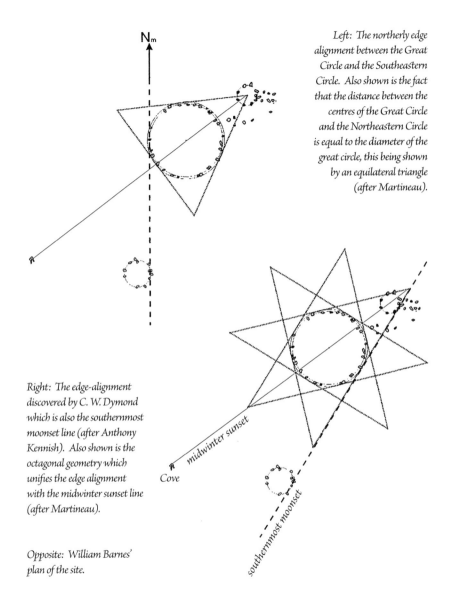

N_m

Left: The northerly edge alignment between the Great Circle and the Southeastern Circle. Also shown is the fact that the distance between the centres of the Great Circle and the Northeastern Circle is equal to the diameter of the great circle, this being shown by an equilateral triangle (after Martineau).

Right: The edge-alignment discovered by C. W. Dymond which is also the southernmost moonset line (after Anthony Kennish). Also shown is the octagonal geometry which unifies the edge alignment with the midwinter sunset line (after Martineau).

Opposite: William Barnes' plan of the site.

Cove

midwinter sunset

southernmost moonset

VANISHED STONES
the lost megaliths

A number of stones from the original design of Stanton Drew are today sadly missing. Specific references are made in the nineteenth century, for example, to 'Tyning's Stones', a pair of megaliths in a field called Middle Ham at Lower Tyning, aligned due west of the Great Circle (*labelled 'Two Stones' on page 250*). Both were reportedly over 5 ft in height, but local sources tell of these two megaliths having been removed in the 1960s. Regrettably, like the Tollhouse Stone, no trace of them remains.

Other stories relate that further stones, particularly from the Great Circle, were destroyed in the medieval period, and in the eighteenth century many were reportedly lost to masonry and road metalling. The later use of Stoney Close (the area containing the Great Circle and the Northeast Circle) as an orchard and for various kinds of farming, would no doubt have caused even further damage.

Despite these trials, however, a good many of the stones of the great circle remain where they fell. A little poking around with a stick on a wet afternoon will enable the keener visitor to discover the outline of some ancient monsters lying just under the turf. Other stones are overgrown but visible. As with Arbor Low, in Derbyshire, one wonders why these fantastic sites are not properly restored and their stones re-erected. Perhaps the authorities are frightened of the magic that might be unleashed if they were.

The pictures opposite are by C. W. Dymond, a civil engineer who made an accurate survey of the stones of Stanton Drew, published in the *British Archaeological Association Journal* of 1877 (*see pages 265–267*).

ESTIMATED ORIGINAL NUMBER OF STONES IN THE CIRCLES.

	MUSGRAVE	STUKELEY	WOOD	RUTTER	WILKINSON	DYMOND
S.W. Circle ...	—	12	12	12	18	12
Great Circle ...	32	30	81	30	38	30 at least
N.E. Circle ...	—	9	8	7	—	8

DIAMETERS OF CIRCLES.

	STUKELEY	WOOD	COLLINSON	SEYER	CROCKER	WILKINSON	DYMOND
S.W. Circle ...	120	140	—	—	129	130	145
Great Circle ...	300	378	300	342	378 × 345	380 × 347	368
N.E. Circle ...	90	96	84	94 to 96	96	c. 96	97

Diameters in feet.

DISTANCES BETWEEN GROUPS.

	WOOD	DYMOND		WOOD	DYMOND
Cove to S.W. Circle ...	—	541.6	Great Circle to N.E. Circle	375	379.8
Cove to Great Circle ...	992	988.0	Great Circle to Quoit ...	c. 1860	c. 1856
S.W. Circle to Great Circle	714	711.6	Great Circle to Two Stones	—	c. 3305

Distances in feet and inches, from centre to centre.

VIEWS AT STANTON DREW, A.D. 1784.

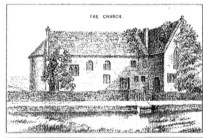

THE CHURCH.

THE DRUIDS' TEMPLE.

THE COVE.

THE DRUIDS' TEMPLE.

J. Jobbins

Mysterious Forces
light phenomena at the stones

Major F.A.Menzies, a distinguished First World War Army engineer and surveyor, claimed he witnessed unusual phenomena at Stanton Drew in the 1940s. Having moved to France to study Feng Shui, he was an established geomancer, reportedly able to locate ley lines and advise on ill health caused by geopathic stress. One day, he had an extraordinary experience which was later related to fellow surveyor, George Sandwich in 1952, a year before his death:

S.T.Loxton

"*Although the weather was dull there was no sign of a storm. Just at a moment when I was re-checking a bearing on one of the stones in that group, it was as if a powerful flash of lightning hit the stone, so the whole group was flood-lit, making them glow like molten gold in a furnace. Rooted to the spot – unable to move – I became profoundly awestruck, as dazzling radiations from above caused the whole group of stones to pulsate with energy in a way that was terrifying. Before my eyes, it seemed the stones were enveloped in a moving pillar of fire – radiating light without heat – writhing upwards towards the heavens: on the other hand it was descending in a vivid spiral effect of various shades of colour – earthward. In fact the moving, flaring lights gyrating around the stones had joined the heavens with the earth.*"

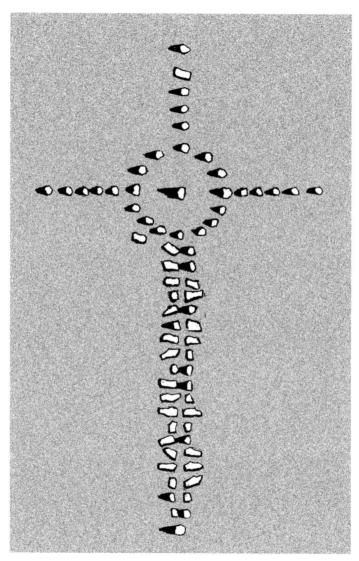

Plan of Callanish from James Logan's The Scottish Gael, *1831.*

CALLANISH

Gerald Ponting

Callanish
←Ring of Brodgar
o Loanhead
of Daviot
o Castlerigg
Arbor
o Low
Rollright
o
Avebury
o
o Stonehenge
Stanton Drew

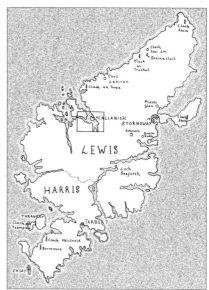

Clach
Stein
Clach
Sgei Lin
Steinacleit
Clach
an
Trushal
Cnoc
Laoiran
Clach an Tursa
Priests
Glen
o CALLANISH
STORNOWAY
Achmore
Braim
Obake
Clach
Stein
LEWIS
Loch
Seaforth
HARRIS
TARBERT
TARANSAY
Clach an
Teampull
Clach Mhicleoid
Borremore
ENSAY

THE OUTER HEBRIDES
Butt of Lewis
LEWIS
Stornoway
CALLANISH
N. HARRIS
Tarbert
HARRIS
N. UIST
Lochmaddy
Balivanick
BENBECULA
S.
UIST
Lochboisdale
BARRA
Castle bay
Barra
Head
20 miles

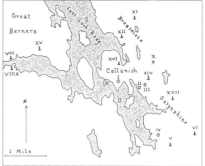

Great
Bernera
East Loch Roog
XI
Breasclete
XII
XV
XVI
X
VIII
Callanish
XIV
VIIIA
II
I
III
XVII
Garynahine
VI
N
IV
V
1 Mile

Sketch of Callanish I, Rev. G. R. Mackarness, 1866

Introduction

Stonehenge is justifiably world-famous, but far to the north in the Outer Hebrides stands a monument just as worthy of attention. Indeed, the Standing Stones of Callanish are sometimes called the 'Stonehenge of the Hebrides'. For visitors who travel to appreciate its grandeur, the site's remoteness adds to its romance.

Callanish and Stonehenge are incredible survivors from a 'megalithic culture' which stretched the length of the British Isles. Brodgar in Orkney, Castlerigg in the Lake District and Rollright in Oxfordshire date from the same prehistoric era, as do around a thousand other stone circles. Many are now ruinous and an unknown number have been lost or destroyed.

Approaching Callanish across the moorlands from Stornoway, the stones appear silhouetted along a ridge. Standing among the stones, the visitor becomes aware of the vast open hemisphere of the sky. There seems little doubt that the Sun and especially the Moon had parts to play in whatever ancient dramas were enacted here.

Callanish is unique among settings of standing stones, having often been compared to the shape of a Celtic cross. Thirteen stones, between 8 and 12 feet tall, form a ring with a maximum diameter of only 41 feet, being slightly flattened on the east side. An impressive megalith, almost 16 feet tall, stands at the centre, set at one end of a burial chamber.

Three rows lead away from the circle, approximately to the east and west, and more precisely to the south. There is also a longer northerly avenue. Three stones are additional to this pattern (*9, 34 and 35, opposite*). The monument measures 400 feet north to south and 150 feet east to west. To the south is the natural rocky outcrop of Cnoc an Tursa.

The standing stones are composed of Lewisian gneiss and may have been transported no more than a mile. The builders probably chose shapes for aesthetic or magical reasons; stones with crystalline nodules were especially favoured.

As this section of *Megalith* reveals, many writers have recorded their opinions about Callanish. However, the motives of those who laboured to create it, perhaps 5,000 years ago, may never be known. Its continuing mystery is part of the attraction of the 'Stonehenge of the Hebrides'.

A NOTE ON PLACE-NAMES. In the text of this book I have used place-names spellings more familiar to English-speaking visitors, with the Gaelic spellings which appear on road signs generally given in brackets. Historic Environment Scotland and the trust which runs the visitor centre use the Gaelic spelling Calanais. However, the name probably originated not in Gaelic but from Old Norse, the language of the Vikings. Kallaðarnes, referred to a 'promontory from which a ferry is called'. Great Bernera was formerly reached by ferry from Callanish.

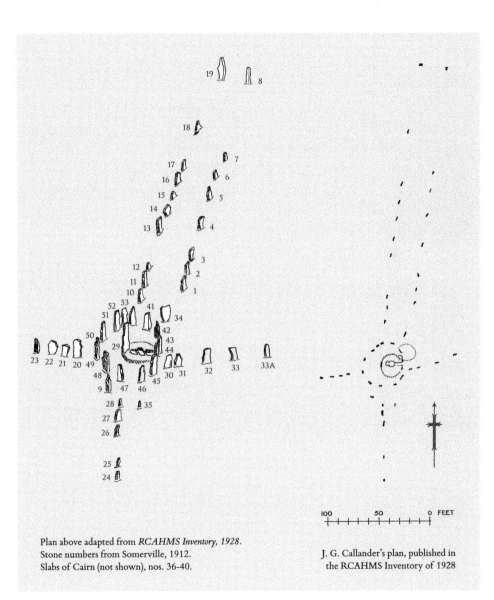

Plan above adapted from *RCAHMS Inventory, 1928.*
Stone numbers from Somerville, 1912.
Slabs of Cairn (not shown), nos. 36-40.

J. G. Callander's plan, published in
the RCAHMS Inventory of 1928

PHASES OF CONSTRUCTION
five thousand years at Callanish

The Isle of Lewis (Leòdhas) seems a remote and unlikely place for prehistoric peoples to have settled. The modern visitor finds stretches of rolling, treeless moorland, inhabited only by hardy black-faced sheep. The coastline varies between spectacular rocky shores and sweeping pristine beaches of white sand. Inland from these beaches, the sandy machair has relatively fertile soil. Most known prehistoric settlement sites, including that at Dalmore (Dail Mhor), nine miles to the north, were on the machair. In Neolithic times, the island was warmer, drier and less windy than today. Sea level was lower, so the sea-loch to the south of Callanish would have been mainly dry land.

A major excavation at Callanish in 1980 and 1981, directed by Patrick Ashmore, identified several phases of activity (*opposite top*): 1. In around 3000 BC early farmers ploughed the soil, which later developed into pasture. 2. A ditch was dug, defining an enclosure which may have been used for ritual purposes. 3. Fourteen megaliths were erected as a circle with a central stone. Small stones and clay were built into a mound around each stone to compensate for the shallowness of the socket holes; the rows may have been added later. 4. The chambers of the cairn were constructed on a specially levelled area, and a circular kerb was added a little later. 5. Later again, perhaps around 1000 BC, the capstones were thrown off the cairn and its contents scattered. Land within the circle was ploughed (maybe a culture with different beliefs had taken over). 6. Strangely, the cairn was then partially rebuilt, using former capstones to make a northern kerb. Not long after this, peat began to form, burying the cairn over the next 3000 years.

Above: The two main phases of building at Callanish (drawings by Patrick Ashmore). The stone circle was erected between 2900 and 2600 BC.

Above: Richly decorated pottery vessels typical of those found at Callanish. Tools were made of bone and stone, with the stone for the axes obtained via far-flung trade routes. One axe, found in the peat in Lewis in 1983, was composed of porcellanite from Ireland with its wooden handle remarkably well preserved (above).

INCHANTERS AND DRUIDS
the earliest writers on Callanish

In *A Description of the Lewis by John Morisone Indweller There*, published around 1680, Callanish was first mentioned in print, though not named:

> '... there are great stones standing up in ranks, some two or three foot thick and 10, 12 and 15 foot high; It is left by traditione that these were a sort of men converted into stones by ane Inchanter ...'

Some twenty years later, in 1703, Martin Martin, a native of Duntulm on the northern tip of the Isle of Skye, published the first plan of the site (*opposite*), in a book titled *A Description of the Western Isles of Scotland*, published in London. It was extremely inaccurate, with far too many stones in the avenue and only three in each of the other rows. His plan did not even match his written description, which gave four stones each in the S, E and W rows.

In his report, Martin reported that local people had claimed that Callanish was

> '... a Place appointed for Worship in the time of Heathenism, and that the Chief Druid or Priest stood near the big Stone in the center, from whence he address'd himself to the People ...'

Later writers repeated Martin's ideas about Druids – and uncritically redrew his plan. The plan appeared in James Logan's *The Scottish Gael* (1831), where although improved in other respects, it still included 19 stones on each side of the avenue (*see page 274*). Years after more accurate material had been published, the plan was still unchanged in Logan's second edition of 1863.

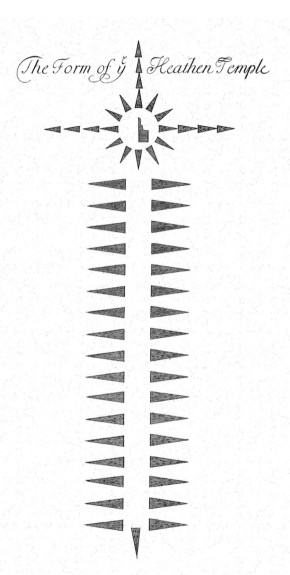

The Form of ẙ Heathen Temple

THE FAMOUS ANTIQUARIAN
Callanish as a 'serpentine temple'

William Stukeley's careful drawings of the great stone circles of Wiltshire, made in the 1720s, are greatly valued today (*see his drawings of Stonehenge on pages 4 and 173, Avebury on pages 194, 207-215, and Stanton Drew on pages 254-257*). Stukeley's later publications are full of fanciful Druid theories, which nevertheless were very influential for many years—indeed he is sometimes regarded as the founder of the druid revival movement. At Avebury, he initially considered the circle and curved avenues to represent a Druidical 'dracontium' or serpentine temple, although he also claimed that it was a symbolic depiction of the Trinity.

The manuscript plan of Callanish (*opposite*) in his *Commonplace Book* was not original, Stukeley never having visited Scotland. He wrote:

'I took a drawing of it from Mr Llwdd's travels but he is a very bad designer ... A part of the snake remains going from it which he calls an avenue. He did not discern the curve of it ...'.

Edward Llwdd (or Lhwyd), whose work is lost, had copied Martin – and it is hardly surprising that he did not notice the curve of the straight Callanish avenue! Stukeley was trying to adjust the facts to fit his theories.

The similarity of the ground plan of Callanish to the shape of a Celtic cross was commented on by Rev. Thomas MacLaughlan in 1863. He speculated that the site was a 'Christian relic', perhaps built as a penance for a grievous sin!

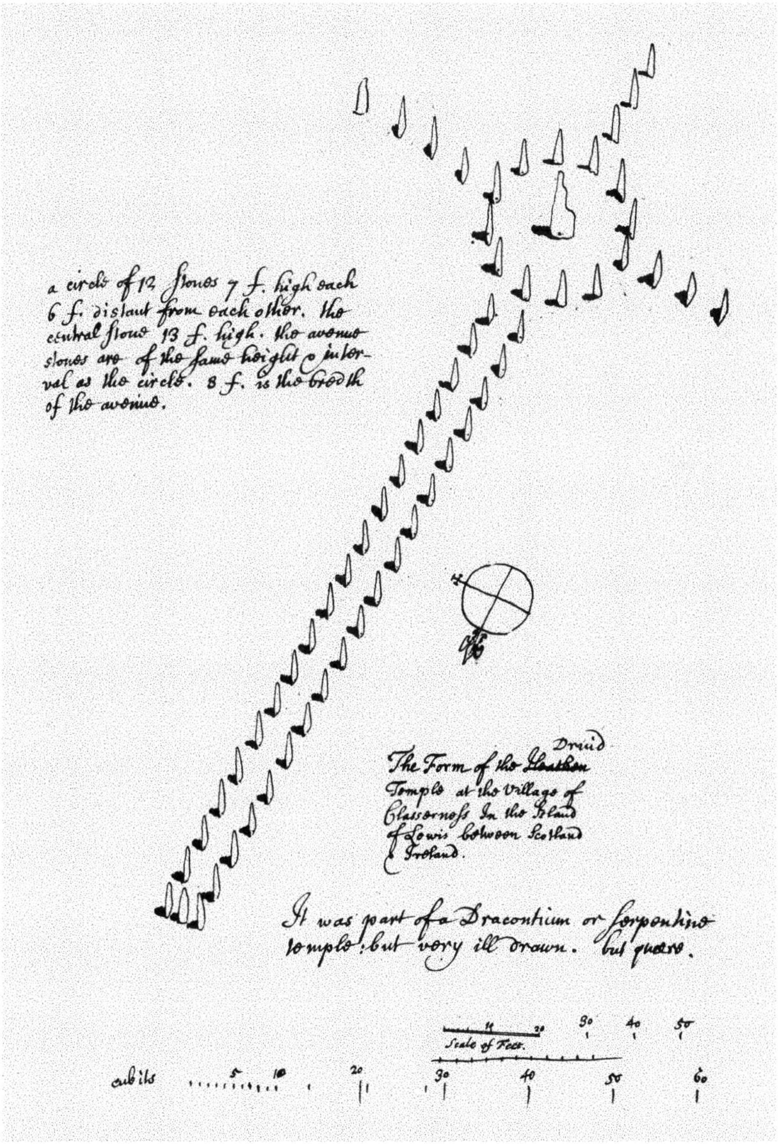
a circle of 12 stones 7 f. high each 6 f. distant from each other. the central stone 13 f. high. the avenue stones are of the same height & inter-val as the circle. 8 f. is the brodth of the avenue.
Druid
The Form of the Heathen Temple at the Village of Classerness In the Island of Lewis between Scotland & Ireland.
It was part of a Dracontium or serpentine temple: but very ill drawn. but quaere.
Scale of Feet.
10 20 30 40 50
cubits 5 10 20 30 40 50 60

A BLANKET OF PEAT
is Callanish a 'restored site'?

By the Iron Age, the climate had deteriorated, and conditions on Lewis were cooler and damper. This resulted in the accumulation of layers of peat, which consists of partially decomposed plant material. By the nineteenth century, much of the island was blanketed in peat to a depth of five or six feet.

At Callanish, the stones thus looked much shorter than they do today. This was reflected in John MacCulloch's plan of 1819 (*opposite*), which shows a number of 'fallen stones'. At least eight of these are standing today, causing later writers to assume their re-erection and to call Callanish a 'restored site'.

MacCulloch's plan has to be interpreted along with drawings made by Tomkin in 1885, after the peat was cleared – but while bleaching of the stones still showed its former depth. Stone 3 had only its top edge exposed in 1819 (*below*) and MacCulloch must have thought he was looking at a much smaller stone, lying on its side. Far from being a restored site, it is now obvious that Callanish was protected, over two or three millennia, by enveloping peat.

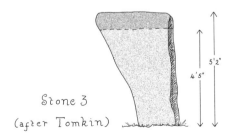

Stone 3
(after Tomkin)

5'2"

4'5"

Feet high

13 ....

7 ....

Druidical Temple in Lewis

8 ....
8 ....

12 ....

Extreme length .... 588'
Interior diameter of circle .. 63
Length from E. to W. 204

feet

with traces of fallen stones 100 feet further.

Scale of Yards.

5   10   20   40

ANTIQUARIANS & ARCHÆOLOGISTS
a helpful Danish visitor

One of the limitations of the early antiquarians was the lack of a chronological framework for the past. Then, in 1851, Daniel Wilson published *Prehistoric Annals of Scotland* (the second edition included an engraving of Callanish, *see page 305, top*). This was the first use of the word 'prehistoric' in English. A Danish professor, Christian Thomsen, had first divided ancient times into Ages of, successively, Stone, Bronze and Iron. So it is perhaps appropriate that the earliest known illustrations of Callanish were drawn by an early archaeologist from Denmark.

A sketch by Jacob Worsaae (*opposite above*), in an 1846 field notebook, confirms the conclusion from the MacCulloch and Tomkin material. Worsaae clearly showed the stones of the circle looking short; he was standing on a ground level five feet higher than today's, due to the blanketing peat.

A second sketch (*opposite below*), looking south towards the circle, shows that the ground level had already been lowered along most of the length of the avenue by peat cutting.

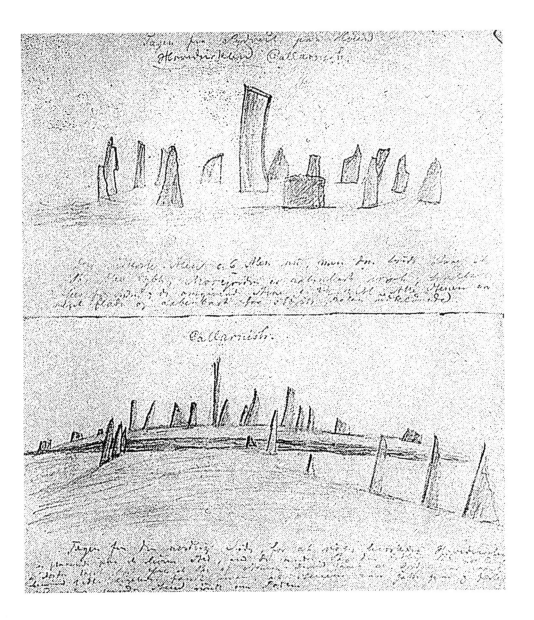

THE 'EXCAVATION' OF 1857
rapid removal of five feet of peat

Henry Callender's paper of 1854 *Notice of the Stone Circle at Callernish* included the 'bird's eye view' (*see page 303, lower*) and a superb engraving by James Kerr (*below*). Villagers are seen gathering fuel by cutting peats across the east row; they could be expected to cut around the circle stones within a few years. Therefore Callender

suggested that the Society of Antiquaries of Scotland should apply to Sir James Matheson, the owner of the Isle of Lewis, for "... the moss to be removed, so as ... to ascertain ... whether any building had been erected at the original level".

The peat was cleared on October 2nd 1857. Cosmo Innes reported to the Society that, five feet down, the workmen came upon "... a chambered building of three compartments".

THE BURIAL CHAMBER
exciting discovery beneath the peat

The discovery of a buried construction at the centre of the Callanish stone circles in 1857 caused quite a stir. The 'chambered building' exactly fitted the small space between the central stone and the eastern-most stones of the circle, as shown in the plan from Innes' paper (*opposite, top*). It was clearly a small burial cairn, surrounded by a circular kerb and containing two roofless compartments and a short passage.

In describing the 1857 'excavation', Sir James Matheson stated:

> "It is remarkable that the sides of the small chamber are quite undisturbed".

(Careful examination in 1981 showed that, in fact, some reconstruction must have taken place, as Victorian glass was found between the stones forming the sides of the chamber.)

With his note, Sir James enclosed

> "... some minute fragments of what we suppose to be bones found
> in the chamber, and a specimen of a black unctuous substance".

A Professor Anderson examined these materials. He concluded that the bones were human, "subjected to the action of fire", but gave no firm opinion about the unctuous substance.

Local tradition tells of village children drawing on the stones with charcoal found at the time. Today's archaeologists inevitably regret that the cairn contents are not available for examination by modern scientific methods.

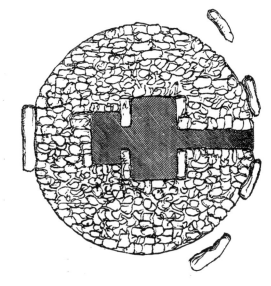

Left: Plan of the chambered cairn found in the Callanish stone circle in 1857, showing how it fits between the central stone on the left, and the eastern curve of the circle on the right.

Left: View into the cairn, clearly showing the three compartments as well as a lintel over one of the doorways.

Two Surveyors and a Vicar

visitors with an artistic eye

With the discovery of the cairn at Callanish in 1857, a visit to the site became a must for all with an interest in the antiquities of Scotland.

Captain F. W. L. Thomas, a prominent member of the Society of Antiquaries, undertook a surveying expedition to Callanish and nearby sites soon after the peat clearance. A fascinating series of delicate pencil drawings of individual stones is attributed to his artist-assistant, known only as 'Mr Sharbau'.

Artistically enhanced copies of Sharbau's faint originals are reproduced overleaf, while his sketch of the cairn appears on the previous page. He used his own numbering system for the stones, but the accepted Somerville numbers replace them here (note that stones 36-40 are not included as they are parts of the cairn.)

Sharbau recorded stone 35 as fallen but it had been re-erected, probably at Matheson's instruction, by the time of Sir Henry James's visit. He was Director-General of the Ordnance Survey and his massive tome *Plans and Photographs of Stonehenge and Tursachan in the Island of Lewis* was published in 1867. It included the most accurate plan of Callanish then available. Of much greater interest today, however, is the attractive 'zincograph' of the circle stones (*opposite top*). Ten years after the acidic peat had been cleared away, its bleaching effect was still clearly visible. This supports all the earlier evidence for the stones having been half-engulfed in five feet of peat. The illustration also shows the cavity of the cairn, but in a 'cosmetically tidy' state.

A modern aquatint by Scottish printmaker Lorraine Tolmie (*lower opposite*) shows how the bleaching effect has since completely faded.

TURUSACHAN, CALLERNISH.
OR
THE PLACE OF PILGRIMAGE ON THE BLEAK HEADLAND.
IN THE
ISLE OF LEWIS.

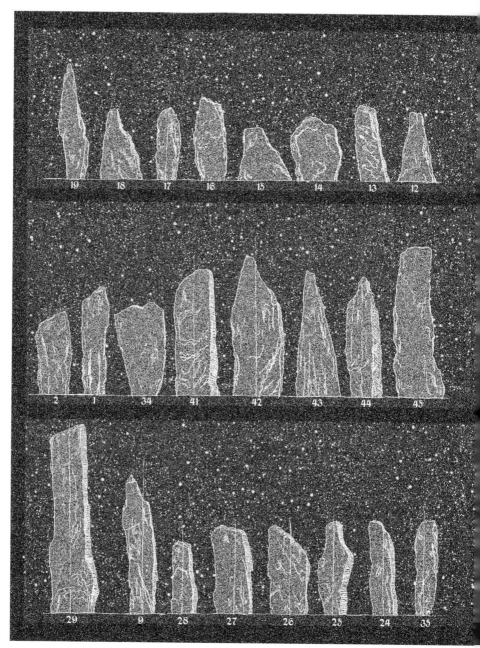

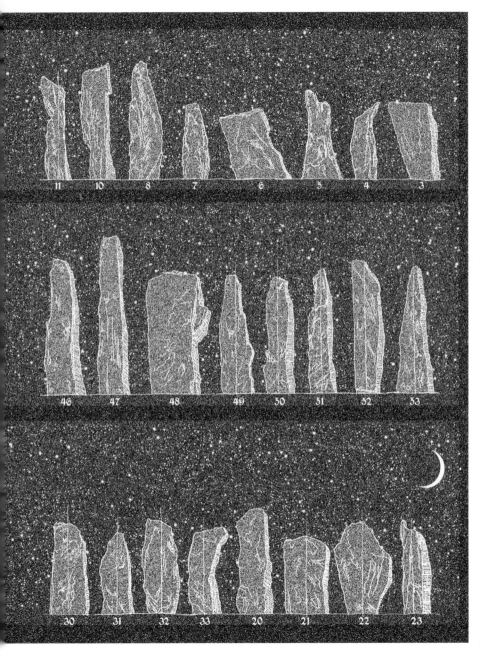

THE PROTECTION OF CALLANISH
the Inspector calls

In order to support Parliamentary approval of an Ancient Monuments Protection Bill, C. P. Kains-Jackson produced *Our Ancient Monuments and the Land Around Them* (1880). This was a descriptive catalogue of important sites throughout Britain which might be scheduled under a new Act. The three-page account of Callanish includes an attractive sketch (*opposite, top*), but with many of the stones drawn out of proportion.

Once the Act was passed, in 1882, General Augustus Pitt Rivers was appointed Inspector of Ancient Monuments. Pitt Rivers could justifiably be called 'the father of British archaeology'. His interest in achaeology began in the 1850s during overseas postings, when he started collecting thousands of ethnographic items, and continued on his return to England, where he performed meticulous and accurately-recorded excavations of many sites on his own Dorset estate. His collection of 22,000 international objects formed the basis of the Pitt Rivers Museum at the University of Oxford. His visit to Lewis in August 1885 marks a turning-point in the story of Callanish. He was accompanied by his artist-assistant, Tomkin (*who drew the sketch opposite below*). As well as a detailed plan they made individual drawings of each stone, showing the former peat level (*example on page 286*). Stone 35, re-erected in the 1860s, was now broken, with the upper half lying alongside the erect stump (*seen in drawing on page 301*). Pitt-Rivers requested its repair, but this was delayed until the 1900s.

In addition, Pitt-Rivers negotiated the future protection of Callanish under the new Act.

Above: View of Callanish from Our Ancient Monuments and the Land Around Them, *C. P. Kains-Jackson, 1880. Below: View of Callanish sketched by Tomkin during a visit with General Augustus Pitt-Rivers, newly appointed Inspector of Ancient Monuments in 1885.*

The Callernish Stones
Isle of Lewis

VISITORS FROM THE CASTLE
eerie noises in the midsummer mist

One of Pitt-Rivers' roles was to persuade landowners to place 'their' monuments under government Guardianship. He had the advantage of being on equal terms with Lady Mary Jane Matheson of Lews Castle, by this time the owner of Lewis. In a letter to Pitt-Rivers she wrote: 'I shall only be too glad to have the Callernish Stones ...put under the Ancient Monts. Act and quite believe it is the only way to preserve them'.

The path seen in John Sinclair's 1891 engraving (*opposite above*) was probably laid for the convenience of house-guests from Lews Castle (Caisteal Leòdhais). A story from this period tells of a visit made by an all-male group to see the midsummer sunrise – girls were not allowed to go, as couples sometimes became engaged at the Stones.

An old Callanish lady, from a family who were 'of the Stones', warned them before they set off that 'only those to whom it is given may see'. Though the weather was clear as the party left and returned to Stornoway (Steòrnabhagh), at Callanish the stones were enveloped in a thick mist, from which eerie noises emerged.

This and other stories and legends were recorded in 1966 by Otta Swire in her book *The Outer Hebrides and Their Legends* (*the illustrations below and lower opposite are both from this book*).

Above: View of Callanish by John Sinclair in 1891, clearly showing the path to the circle, and the bleaching of the lower half of the stones. Below: Illustration of Callanish from The Outer Hebrides and Their Legends, *1966, by Otta Swire.*

LEGENDS OF THE STONES
cuckoos, wrens, witches and a magic cow

A legend common to many British circles is that the megaliths are people who were turned to stone for some transgression. At Callanish, the story is that St Kieran literally petrified pagan giants who were meeting to oppose Christianity. The adaptation opposite of James's engraving (*page 295*) in the library of St Andrew's University shows the stones of the circle as anthropomorphic figures, while short stone 30 becomes a seat for a fiddler. The Gaelic word for the standing stones, Tursachan or Turusachan, is often taken to mean 'place of sadness'.

Several tales involve birds: the first cuckoo of Spring traditionally gave its first call from the stones. A cuckoo's call also heralded the mysterious 'Shining One' who is said to have walked up the avenue at midsummer sunrise. Wrens always flew alongside the chief priest, who wore a cloak of coloured feathers. He and his fellow priests were supposed to have originally brought the stones to Lewis in many ships.

In another story a Gaelic-speaking cow came to the stones during a famine and gave milk to all, but a witch used a bottomless bucket to milk her dry. The cow was not seen again.

Another legend tells of a local girl who asked a witch for a magical belt to harm her rival in love. Thinking better of this evil act she disposed of the belt by wrapping it around one of the stones. At once the stone was enveloped in flames and broke in two, amid noises of howling and flapping wings.

At Beltane (traditionally May 1st) tradition was that all fires were to be extinguished on the island. An old priest then produced fire from a nearby tree and redistributed it from within the circle.

TURUSACHAN CALLERNISH

AS SEEN UNDER THE INFLUENCE OF SPIRITS

Above: The stones of Callanish as giants, petrified when the music stopped.
Below: Survey of Callanish from Henry Callendar's paper of 1854.

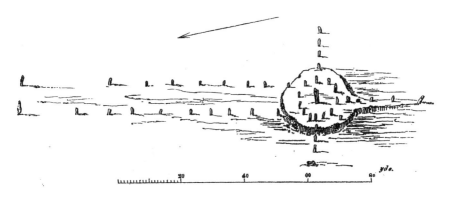

Beyond the Fringe
the Sleeping Beauty as the White Goddess

A range of hills in south-east Lewis takes on the appearance of a supine woman only when seen from the Callanish area (*see below*). She is called the Sleeping Beauty and, less flatteringly, Cailleach na Mointeach, 'the old woman of the moors'.

The idea that this 'figure' had a connection with the Callanish sites arose out of astronomical research by Margaret Curtis and myself. At significant times in the lunar cycle, the Moon rises from this part of the southern horizon (*see pages 312-313*).

Esoteric researchers have enthusiastically adopted the Sleeping Beauty as a representation of the 'White Goddess' or the 'universal Earth Mother'. Some believe that ceremonies relating to birth, fertility and death took place in the Callanish circle - rousing the White Goddess and revitalising the island and its people.

For a certain type of visitor, stone circles emanate an indefinable mystical aura, perhaps captured in Gail Kelly's artistic interpretation of Ceann Hulavig (*Callanish IV, opposite, below*).

THEORIES ABOUT CALLANISH
a 'rude astronomical observatory'?

Callanish has been explained in many ways. Different writers said that it was the 'supreme court of the Hebridean monarch', a resting place of the illustrious dead, an ancient gothic court, or a temple to Thor or Apollo. To many it was 'the great Druidical Cathedral of Scotland'. In 1831, Logan imagined Scottish Druids as seen below, but the cult probably never reached the Hebrides. In any case, stone circles were built at least a millennium before the time of the Druids.

John Toland suggested in 1726 that the 'twelve obelisks of the circle' represented the signs of the Zodiac while the 'nineteen stones on each side of the avenue' related to the 19-year lunar cycle. The stone rows related to the four principal winds.

In 1808, James Headrick called Callanish a 'rude astronomical observatory' where priests marked out the rising of the Sun, Moon and stars. Henry Callender claimed that the south row and the central pillar lined up with the Pole Star – but there was no star in that position in Neolithic times.

These early suggestions that there was a connection between Callanish and the heavens foreshadowed a more scientific approach to astronomy and the stones in the twentieth century. Sir Norman Lockyer, working from previous studies in 1909, claimed to have discovered two star alignments, but few researchers accept alignments with stars today.

ASTRONOMY AT THE STONES
Admiral Somerville and Professor Thom

Admiral Boyle Somerville surveyed Callanish and in 1912 published the most accurate plan up to that date (*opposite*). His numbering of the stones remains in use today (*pages 279, 296–297*). Of the astronomical alignments which he claimed, the most significant was the line from stone 9 to stone 34, which 'points' to the moonrise at its furthest north. This was the first suggestion that prehistoric man might have followed the complex movements of the Moon.

Alexander Thom, a Professor of Engineering at Oxford, spent many years surveying standing stone sites throughout Britain. The original observation which stimulated his interest was made on a summer evening in 1923, when he had anchored his yacht near Callanish. Decades later, he explained:

> '… after dinner, we went ashore to explore … I saw by looking at the Pole Star that there was a north/south line in the complex … I wondered whether the alignment … had been deliberately built that way …'

Thom's eventual conclusions, which created a furore in archaeology, were that the builders of stone circles used the same system of measurement and geometry throughout Britain and that they possessed a detailed knowledge of astronomy. See his survey of Callanish I (*inset*).

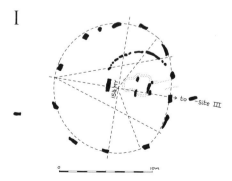

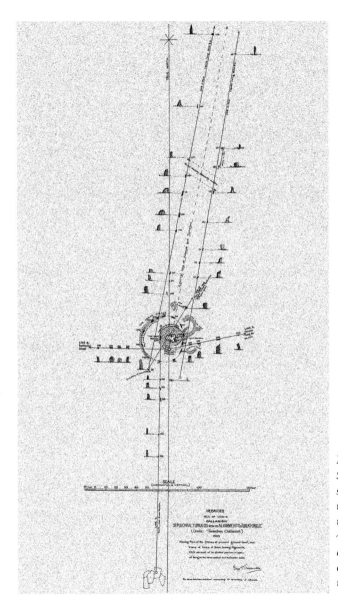

Left: Admiral Boyle Somerville's 1912 survey of Callanish, the most accurate at that time. Somerville was the first person to connect the site with extreme northerly moonrises.

MEGALITHIC SCIENCE
measurement, geometry and astronomy

Only some 'stone circles' are truly circular, like that at Achmore (*opposite*). Aubrey Burl suggests these may be the earliest sites. Alexander Thom concluded that many others were constructed in geometrical shapes. He classified the central circle at Callanish as a Type-A Flattened Circle. Callanish II and Callanish X also fit the same geometry, while sites II and IV are both ellipses.

Thom theorised that the circle builders used a unit equal to 2.72 feet, naming it the Megalithic Yard. According to Ron Curtis's survey, Callanish IV has a long axis of 15 MY, a short axis of 12 MY and a perimeter of just over 42½ MY.

Although Thom's specific ideas on astronomy at Callanish have been largely superseded, his books stimulated the new discipline of archaeoastronomy. Stone alignments are checked to see if the ancient builders lined them up with prominent horizon features where the Sun or Moon rose or set, either at their extreme positions, or at the time of significant calendrical events.

DETAILS OF THE SIX SURVEYS SHOWN OPPOSITE:

Achmore - after Ponting.

Site I - after Thom's version of Somerville's survey. Geometry from Curtis.

Sites II, III and IV - Compound images, after Curtis and Thom.

Site X - Survey and geometry after Curtis.

Arrows indicate Curtis's suggested inter-site alignments.

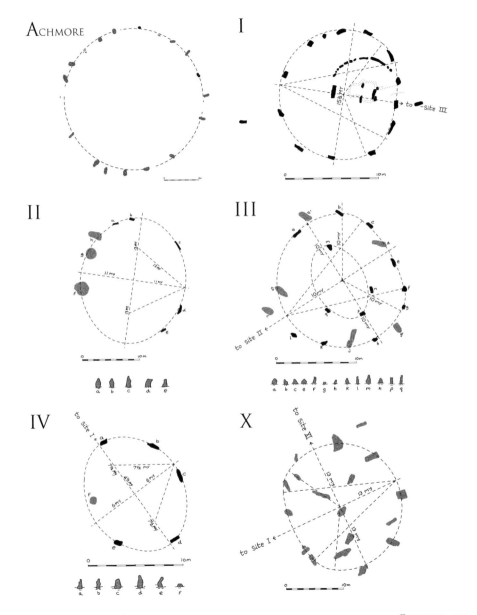

ACHMORE

I

II

III

IV

X

PREHISTORIC TEMPLES
why were stone circles built?

At the northerly latitude of Callanish, every year the sunrise swings from 40° at midsummer to 140° at midwinter, more than in southern England. The Moon's rising and setting positions on the horizon undergo a similar variation over each lunar month, but the extent of the swing around the horizon varies over a cycle lasting 18.6 years (*see pages 166–169*). The largest lunar swings are from 23° to 157°, and occur at the 'major standstills', as in 2006 and 2025, when the Moon rises and sets further north and south than the Sun ever reaches. At the latitude of Callanish, this event is especially spectacular, as the southernmost Moon barely skims the southern horizon (*see below*).

'Primitive' cultures tend to combine all aspects of their lives— religion, art, medicine, astronomy and farming—in a single ritual framework. Construction of a circle must have been a communal effort which aided social cohesion. When complete, it was probably a social and religious centre with purposes not dissimilar to those of a medieval parish church. Whatever deity was worshipped, ceremonies

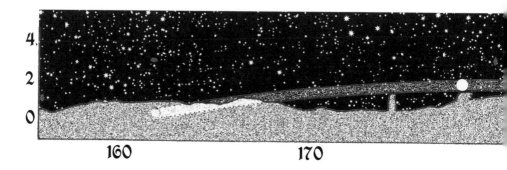

in the circle probably included harvest celebrations, initiation, fertility and funeral rites, even trading. Officiating 'priests' may have had detailed knowledge of the movements of the Sun and Moon, handed down as oral tradition and preserved in megalithic structures. Thus the best times for impressive ceremonies would have been known.

Two classical Greek writers wrote about the northern region of 'Hyperborea'. Eratosthenes said the Hyperboreans' temple was 'winged', while in 55 BC Diodorus wrote:

> '…there is also on the island … a notable temple which is … spherical in shape … the Moon, as viewed from this island, appears but a little distance from the earth … the god visits the island every nineteen years…'

The facts fit Callanish well. For spherical, read circular, while the east and west rows could be the 'wings'; 19 years is close enough to 18.6; for the god, read the Moon, which does remain 'a little distance from the earth' at its southern extreme.

In September 2006, observers standing in the avenue witnessed this extreme lunar event as the Moon rose out of the Sleeping Beauty, skimmed the horizon, and set briefly, before re-appearing 'among' the stones of the circle.

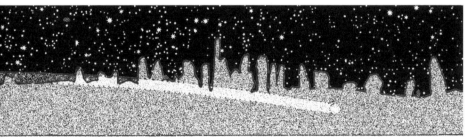

190   200

CNOC CEANN A' GHARRAIDH
Callanish II

At the end of a cul-de-sac road, about half a mile to the south-west of Callanish, stands another fascinating circle of stones, often referred to as 'Callanish II'. Its Gaelic name, pronounced approximately 'croc kyain a gaa-ree', means 'the hillock at the end of the wall'. There are five erect stones, one almost ten feet high, plus four or more fallen slabs.

As the 'minor site' nearest the 'main site', this circle was recorded by several antiquarian visitors. After the success of the peat clearance at the main Callanish site, Sir James Matheson had the peat cleared from sites II, III and IV in the following year. (*See location map, page 276*).

John Stuart's bird's eye view drawing (*shown opposite*) clearly shows a cairn and other internal features which were revealed in 1858, shortly before his visit. Stuart's paper was called *Notes of Incised Marks on one of a Circle of Standing Stones*. He believed, rather gullibly, that a particular stone was marked with deliberate characters, perhaps even Ogham script! Undoubtedly, these were naturally occurring cracks. (It is the rounded stone, lying a little below the centre of the circle.) The stone is said to have been moved to Sir James's estate in Stornoway for protection. If so, it was later partially broken up as building material.

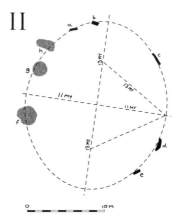

1. Stone with supposed Inscription on its side.
2. Cairn or heap of small stones.
3, 4, 5, 6. Small pits in which charcoal was found.
7, 8. Flat stones.

W. & A.K. Johnston, Edinburgh.

BIRDS EYE SKETCH OF STANDING STONES

About a mile from the large stone Circle near Callernish Island of Lewis.

CALLANISH III & IV
Cnoc Fillibhir Bheag & Ceann Hulavig

The Gaelic name of Callanish III, pronounced 'croc filiver vegg', means little Fillivir hillock. Eight stones stand erect, with another four standing within the ring, as shown in Admiral Somerville's survey (*opposite, above*). There are also several fallen stones.

Clearly visible from the road when approaching Callanish from Stornoway, it is the most visited of the so-called minor sites. In modern times, the circle seems to attract the more mystically-inclined visitor, who may regret the modern intrusion of interpretive notices and a hard surrounding path at Callanish itself. On a stormy winter day in 1984, the Glaswegian rock band, 'Ultravox', made a pop video here.

About 1¼ miles south lies Ceann Hulavig ('kyain hoo-la-vig', head of Hula bay, Callanish IV). The site is accessed from the Garynahine-Uig road by a path and gate. Its five tall stones are all encrusted with hoary lichen, standing on an ellipse (*see too etching on page 305*).

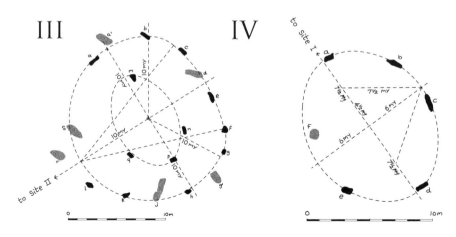

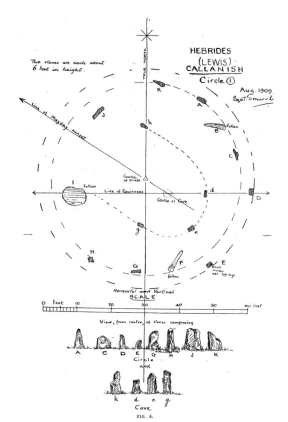

Left: Admiral Somerville's 1912 survey of Callanish III. Somerville, fascinated by standing stones, devoted much of his spare time from 1908 until his death surveying ancient sites and was one of the early pioneers of archaeoastronomy.

Below: Callanish IV. When peat was removed here in the late 1850s only the area within the stones was cleared, with the result that they stand around a poorly-drained hollow, as shown in Tomkin's sketch.

Connections Between Sites
reasons for numerous sites in one area

Why are so many standing stone sites concentrated around Callanish, and what was the connection between them? There are various suggestions.

→ The sites are of different periods, each being constructed as an improvement upon the previous one.

→ Each site was the temple of a branch of the ancient religion, in the same way that each Christian sect has its own churches.

→ Each circle was the focus of a small community. This has been shown to be likely in, for example, the Lands End area. If each small ring was, in episcopalian terms, a 'parish church', then Callanish itself must have been the 'cathedral'.

→ All the sites were in use at the same time and formed an interdependent complex, perhaps with sight-lines between them having astronomical significance. This idea is implicit in the concept of the 'Callanish diamond' (*opposite*), with all the sites being in an area where two ranges of hills relate to the rise and set of the Moon at its most extreme southerly position.

Callanish still keeps many of its secrets, despite the best efforts of eighteenth and nineteenth century antiquarians and twentieth century archaeologists and astronomers. The techniques of the future may reveal some of the site's mysteries, but will not destroy the fascination of 'the Stonehenge of the Hebrides'.

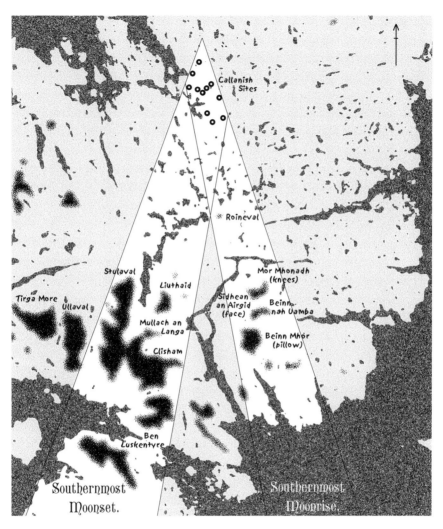

Above: When the Moon at its southernmost extreme rises over the hills of the
Sleeping Beauty and sets into the Harris hills, the viewing lines for moonrise and
moonset form a 'diamond', within which all the Callanish sites lie. Could
this be the reason why so many sites are found in this area?

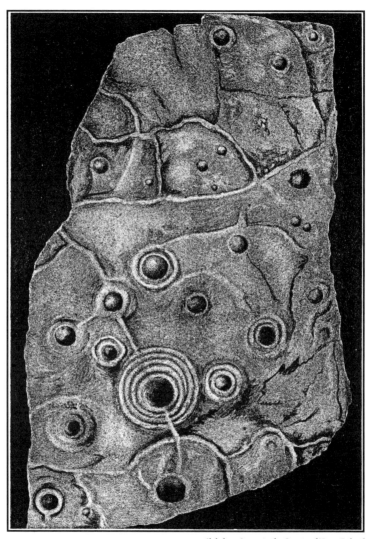

Slab from Sneem in the County of Kerry, Ireland

ANCIENT BRITISH
ROCK ART

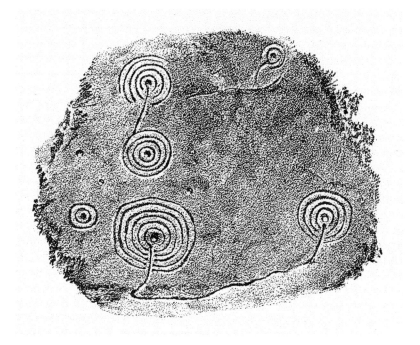

Chris Mansell

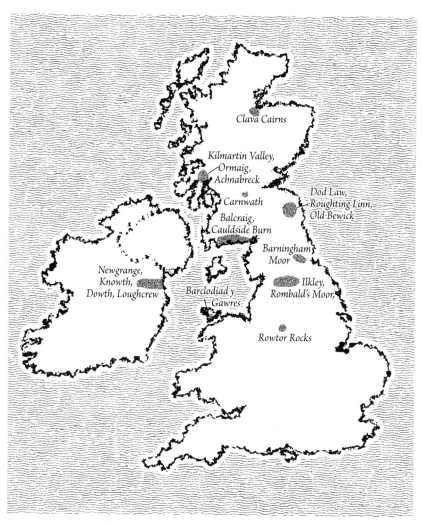

Some important sites mentioned in the text.

Introduction

Sitting on a hillside at one particularly extensive site near Kilmartin, early on a warm summer's morning, waiting for the Sun to rise above the pine forest and illuminate the wonderful range of carvings, I realised that there may never be any explanation for these ancient designs. I often feel that my own involvement with this subject is as much of a mystery as the images themselves. However, perhaps we are often so preoccupied with the process of rationalisation that we lose sight of our original attraction and involvement, which was, for me, largely aesthetic. On this occasion the simple fact of being in this remote and beautiful place, with these mysterious images, was explanation enough.

The Kilmartin Valley, in Argyllshire, is only one of many sites in Great Britain and Ireland which exhibit ancient rock carvings. Having visited this area some years earlier without time to explore some of the more remote sites I had always intended to return. There is, simply, a treasure chest of prehistoric features with decorated burial chambers, standing stones, stone alignments and circles and a wealth of rock carvings. It is almost like a gazetteer of the finest evidence of our ancient culture.

In Northumberland, Durham, Yorkshire, Derbyshire, Galloway in Scotland and in County Meath in Ireland there are also extensive examples of carvings displaying many different styles. It seems somewhat surprising that, while so much is made of the cave paintings at Altamira in Spain and at Lascaux in France, in our own environment exist some of the most mysterious, enigmatic and beautiful designs which, until fairly recent times, have gone largely unnoticed.

I can't remember exactly how I came to be aware of ancient rock carvings. I was born and lived in Durham for many years, totally unaware that within an hour's drive were excellent examples of prehistoric art, at Dod Law, Old Bewick and Roughting Linn in Northumberland, and at Barningham Moor in County Durham, I can only say that my joy at their discovery and my subsequent involvement has led me to an area of research which gives me continuous pleasure.

As an artist myself, my interest in rock art is largely visual, I do not claim to be an archaeological historian, but, as this seems to be a visual language, I think we can look at them as we would any other work of art. I have been significantly inspired and fascinated by the research of people such as Stan Beckensall, Michael J. O'Kelly and Martin Brennan, and by organisations like the Ilkley Archaeology Group, the Royal Commission on the Ancient and Historic Monuments of Scotland, the Kilmartin House Museum and the Newgrange Museum in Ireland. If it was not for the excellent work and contribution of people such as these the subject would hardly be in evidence.

These pages mainly covers examples of carvings from Great Britain and Ireland, but it is worth mentioning that rock art exists all over the world. For me these drawings have a particular mystery and visual beauty which is impossible to assess, evidence of a bygone intelligence and culture, and it gives me great pleasure to share with those who look at this section some of that mystery and some of the time I have spent with this fascinating subject.

Cairn L, Loughcrew, Co Meath.

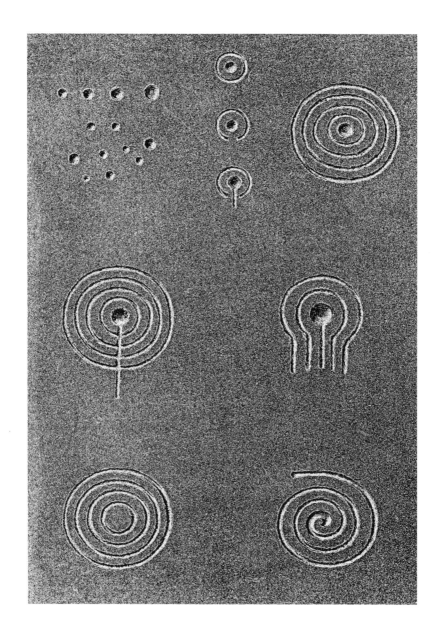

DISTRIBUTION OF ROCK ART
an overview of primary sites and styles

The formal elements of rock carvings exhibit many different styles. The most important sites covered in the text are shown in the map opposite page 1.

Locations often have similar types of carvings but also display unique drawings. Likewise, there is no hard and fast rule for the surfaces employed, but examples from Northern England and Scotland generally seem to occur on natural horizontal outcrops, while in Ireland and Anglesey the carvings appear on the walls of passage graves, or on

individual vertical stones.

Many of the carvings found in passage graves are quite ornate, involving spirals and complex designs, while those on outdoor horizontal surfaces tend to involve cups and rings and more basic patterns.

Individual elements such as cups and sets of rings are usually fairly small, ranging from one to eight inches in diameter. However, multiple arrangements of carvings can cover many square yards as can be seen at Achnabreck in the Kilmartin Valley.

The drawings are thought to have been created by the process of "pecking", gradually chipping away the surface with a stone chisel from a basic scratch to a depth of about one inch.

Roughting Linn, Northumberland

ROUGHTING LINN
Northumberland

The carvings shown here are from Roughting Linn, one of the largest known decorated outcrops, which exhibits a range of complex designs developed largely around the 'cup and ring' format. The illustration of the site on the previous page, produced for the Duke of Northumberland in 1869, shows the site as a bleak and remote outcrop in the middle of extensive moorland, a majestic feature in an empty landscape.

Today the site is bypassed by a road. Trees and bushes have grown up and it has been surrounded by a fence. It might seem that much of its original aesthetic relationship with the landscape has been lost, but, judging by the quantity of small offerings on view at every visit, this place is still special to many.

The sheer scale of Roughting Linn is testament to the fact that whoever produced these drawings was making a deliberate and significant statement.

CUPS AND RINGS
the basic motifs

"Cups and rings" is a generic term for a whole range of Neolithic and Bronze Age rock carvings dated to 2000–3000 BC.

In truth the simple phrase belies a whole range of styles and designs which have interested and intrigued researchers and enthusiasts since the last century. There are many different combinations of design elements to be found, and the existence of anomalies, such as the "ladder" forms found on Rombald's Moor, confounds the notion of an over-arching explanation.

Different sites throughout the British Isles also often exhibit specific innovations and motifs which may possibly be explained by influences from differing cultures, but the cup-and-ring format seems to be a common thread. Many of the carvings are linked to contemporary cairns and burial mounds, but others can be found isolated on remote outcrops on empty moorland.

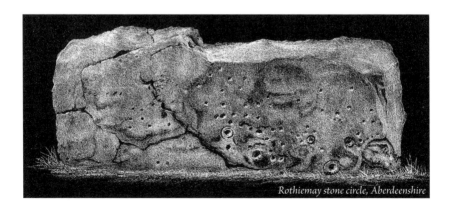

Rothiemay stone circle, Aberdeenshire

Craigie Hill

EARLY AND MODERN RESEARCH
from the 1860s until the present

It seems strange that the subject of ancient British rock art is so roundly ignored by the contemporary art world. We have to go back over 100 years, to the mid 19th century, before we find the last flurry of interest.

In the 1860s a rash of publications appeared with detailed lithographs and drawings of these fascinating forms; there were books by G. Tate, Sir J. Y. Simpson and, at the request of the Duke of Northumberland, a large format series of plates based on surveys by J Collingwood Bruce. Popular interest spiked again in the 1880s before going underground in the 20th century.

In recent years the hard work and perseverance of Stan Beckensall has generated and maintained an interest in the subject and his considerable work in recording and archiving many carvings will long benefit others.

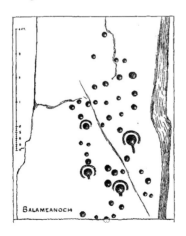

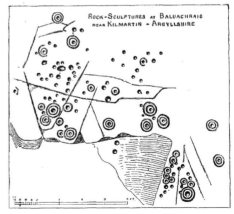

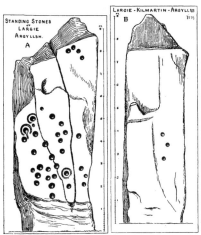

STANDING STONES of LARGIE ARGYLLSH. A

LARGIE · KILMARTIN · ARGYLL B

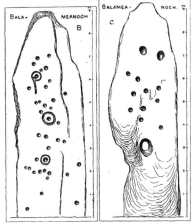

BALA · MEANOCH B

BALAMEA · NOCH. C

CUP-MARKED STONE – WELTON · FORFAR.

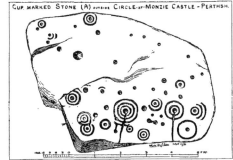

CUP·MARKED STONE (A) OUTSIDE CIRCLE-AT-MONZIE CASTLE · PERTHSH.

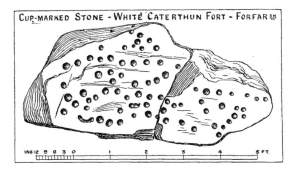

CUP-MARKED STONE – WHITE CATERTHUN FORT – FORFAR.

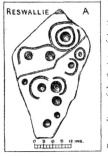

RESWALLIE A

CUP MARKINGS
Clava Cairns, Invernesshire

The Clava Cairns, or Bulnaraun of Clava, consist of three cairns, two of which have passageways aligned to the southwestern midwinter sunset position. They may be found down a minor road off the B9006 from Inverness.

Cup marks are clearly visible on some of the stones, and their deliberate inclusion and arrangement within the overall design and structure of the site is strong evidence for their possessing some kind of significance and meaning.

The Clava Cairns group is one of the best examples of a Bronze Age burial complex in Scotland, each of the three cairns here being surrounded by a stone circle. The cup marks are to be found on the outer facing stones of the cairns, but it has been suggested that the carvings may be even older than the structure, the stones having been reused because of their special status.

Oakland circle

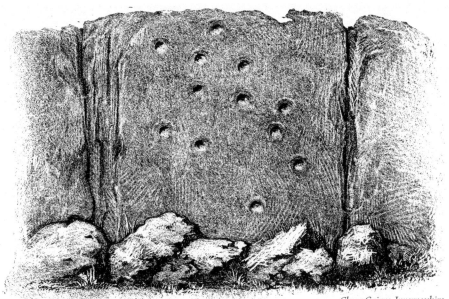

Clava Cairns, Invernesshire

Clava Cairns, Invernesshire

Joined Cups
Rosshire fragments

The joining together of discrete visual elements with varying types of pathway is a development seen at many locations (e.g., Ormaig and Old Bewick) and it is clear that there is some intention here in relating one element to another.

Cups and rings are also commonly found on horizontal outcrops, which has prompted suggestions that these joined motifs were used for water or blood in ritual processes in some way. However, at Ballochmyle in Ayrshire the carvings are found on a cliff face, so this would seem to contradict that theory. It is additionally possible that some symbolic connection is being made between the joined elements.

Ratho

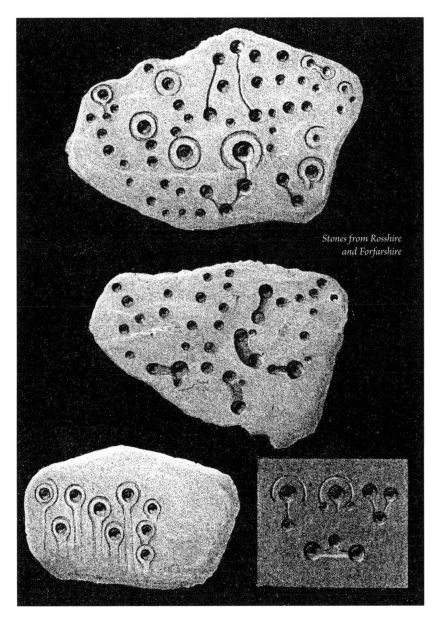

Stones from Rosshire and Forfarshire

Ringed Cups

Ballymenach Stones, Kilmartin Valley, Argyllshire

This site consists of an alignment of quite large standing stones, averaging about twelve feet, one being extensively decorated with cup and ring markings. There is a kerb cairn and a henge nearby. A modern drawing with more detail than the 19th century lithograph opposite is shown below.

It is impossible to tell whether these remaining stones were part of a larger arrangement, but they are somewhat reminiscent of the stone avenue at Avebury. The decorated stone is immediately significant in the sense that the carvings are not made on a horizontal surface as are the majority of examples in this area. It has therefore been suggested that the carvings may predate the stone's erection here, posing the question of its positional importance in relationship to its neighbours. The alignment is north-south.

The concept of the carvings being applied to a vertical stone would be evidence for the merging of two different processes, signs of which also occur nearby at Nether Largie.

Ballymenach Stones, Kilmartin Valley, Argyllshire

Standing stones at Ballymenach, Argyllshire

ENCLOSED CUPS & RECTANGLES
Dod Law, Northumberland & Rowtor Rocks, Derbyshire

The area surrounding Dod Law shows a great variety of carvings, once again on flat outcrops on the highest ground. The rectangular detail on the stone opposite does not include rings as a formal element and is an interesting diversion. There is reasonable evidence here to suggest the more diagrammatic or representational purpose of these designs. The motif could possibly relate to the plans of an enclosure or hillfort.

The pattern below, from Rowtor Rocks, interestingly includes cups and rings along with the visually more complex carving of the petalled form. The radiating elements could relate to organic matter or may represent the rays of the sun. The design is also reminiscent of a plan of the great Derbyshire fallen stone circle at Arbor Low.

Dod Law

THE CALDERSTONES
Allerton, Liverpool

The Calderstones are the remains of a Neolithic passage grave which was destroyed in 1845. They were placed on display close to the entrance to Liverpool's Calderstones Park at the time, and were then moved again in 1964 and set in a circle.

A range of elements found in rock art appear here, including carved footprints which are more common in Scandinavia and Brittany and rare in the United Kingdom.

The main motifs are cups, concentric rings, concentric rings with central cups and spirals. The spirals are both clockwise and anti-clockwise; there is some suggestion, from examples at Newgrange, that this could record some seasonal change.

It is not unreasonable to suspect that something is being recorded here and that the different combinations of symbols may have specific meanings. Likewise, the various number of cups at different sites may record different quantities.

Dorsetshire

The Calderstones, now in a glasshouse in Liverpool

BALLYGOWAN CARVINGS
near Slockavullin, Kilmartin Valley, Argyllshire

Ballygowan is one of a number of sites in the Kilmartin Valley which display considerable and complex arrangements of rock carvings. As at West Horton in Northumberland (*below*) the carvings mainly consist of cups, rings, tails and pathways but also, similarly, there are occasional anomalies such as the small horseshoe labyrinth in the bottom left of the picture (*opposite*). Some of these small elements appear so rarely that they can be considered as being specific to the site, making it even more difficult to propose a consistent explanation for these carvings.

Most of the sites in the Kilmartin area are easily accessed and well worth a visit.

West Horton, Northumberland

TAILS
Achnabreck and Cairnbaan, Argyllshire

So far we have seen cups and rings mainly existing either alone or in combination. It is time to introduce another interesting element, the "tail". These examples from the Kilmartin Valley show tails which extend from central cups or from the inner ring. They may join cups, pair as two tails, or join other tails, but in all of these examples the tail cuts through the rings. At other sites (e.g., Millstone Burn in Northumberland) the rings are even truncated to allow the tail to pass through.

In the example from Cairnbaan (*opposite top*), the tails vary in the way in which they interact with the cups and rings, possibly revealing some function in the style of the tail itself. Some tails are straight and others are curved. One set of rings opposite has two tails which extend and join to enclose a single cup. These are unlikely to be arbitrary decisions and seem to indicate some specific intention.

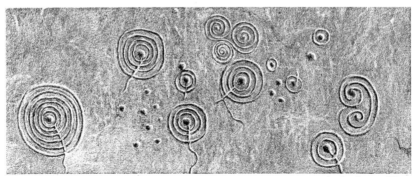

Achnabreck, Argyllshire

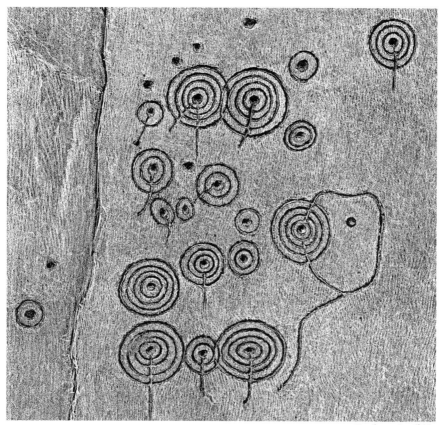

Carnbaan, Argyllshire

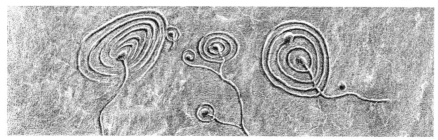

Achnabreck, Argyleshire

TAILED CUPS WITH RINGS
a range of examples

The tailed cup is a prominent design element in many areas. Shown here are examples from a further range of sites. The tail gives the simple cup mark some kind of development, a movement from inside to outside, a bridge, perhaps between one dimension and another. The rings opposite are not broken, in contrast to other examples (*below left*) which allow the tail to pass through. The multiple rings help to intensify the central cup and create a more powerful design.

Evidence from Irish passage grave sites suggests that pictograms were linked with astronomical phenomena. Are these records of years perhaps, or moons? Shown on this page are tailed cups with 1, 2, 3, 4, 5, 6, 7 and 8 rings. In the examples from Achnabreck and Millstone Burn one may notice that the tails all have the same general direction. Could this be some kind of indication of movement?

Millstone Burn, Northumberland   *Balcraig, Galloway*

Achnabreck, Argyllshire

Coverstone of a cist, Coilsfield, Ayrshire,

Cups, Rings and Ladders
Panorama and Barmishaw stones, Ilkley, W. Yorks.

The Panorama Stone was named after the area where it was found on the edge of Rombald's Moor. The first recorded recognition of the carvings on this site was in 1850. Shortly after its discovery in 1871 by a Mr. Call and a Mr. Wagstaff, the stone was sold to a local doctor for preservation. It now stands inside railings opposite St. Margaret's Church in Ilkley. One of the best examples of the "ladder" motif, unique to this area (*see too the Barmishaw Stone below*), it is interesting to follow the structure of the design and see how the ladders, rings and cups form the overall construction. The ladder obviously adds another ingredient to our pot.

Barmishaw Stone,
Rombald's Moor

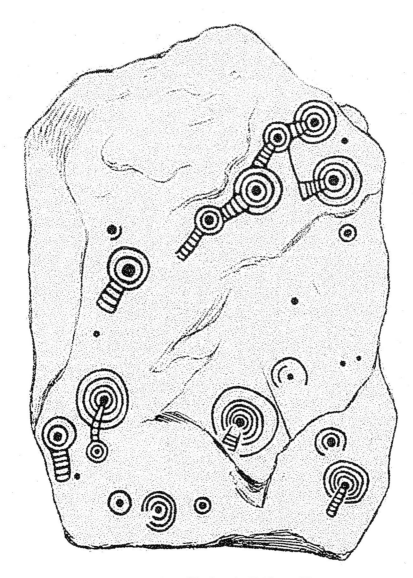

Panorama Stone, Ilkley, drawn by J R Allen in 1879.

Rosette Wheels with Cups
Ormaig, Argyllshire

The complex and diverse arrangement of carvings on the facing page was revealed after a great deal of time spent carefully brushing away a thick layer of pine needles.

There are two main outcrops at this location, which is probably best known for the "rosette" design (*below*). A good mixture of styles is present and some unusual "beak" motifs are attached to cups and rings. Some of the carvings are quite deep, up to one and a half inches, and the larger rings measure about a foot in diameter. This site now lies in a small clearing, deep in the forest, and is not easy to find without some direction as many of the forest roads have been relocated.

The rosette design is interesting in the fact that seven and eleven cups are enclosed and separated in this specific style. This poses the question of the significance of these numbers and what informed these decisions.

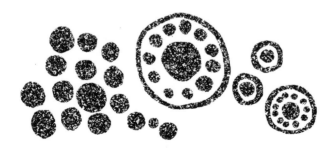

Ormaig, Argyllshire

DECORATED STONES
Long Meg, Cumbria & Barningham Moor, Co. Durham

Long Meg is one of the largest stone circles in the British Isles and Meg, the single outlier (*shown opposite*), marks the midwinter sunset position. The carvings are faint and best observed in glancing light, or at night with the use of a lantern.

The design shown below is a fascinating arrangement of cups, rings and adjoining pathways, and evokes all kinds of explanations. Perhaps there is evidence here of some ritual which has been long forgotten. The carvings are weathered and heather obscures many of the stones scattered over the moor.

The nature of the location must always be a consideration in studying and comparing styles and variations in different areas of rock art, and here the location and weathering of the examples seems to enhance the overall quality of this bleak environment.

Barningham Moor, Co. Durham

Long Meg, Cumbria

NORTHUMBRIAN DETAILS
from Dod Law, and Horton Moor

These images from the mid 19th century were originally printed using a specialist lithographic technique which employed a Balkan limestone as a printing surface. It seems appropriate that a stone process was used here to reproduce ancient marks made on stone.

The designs, from Dod Law and Horton Moor, are complex, playful and varied. A vulva-like shape (*opposite top right*), comb-like forms (*opposite lower right*) and a splayed-ringed cup (*opposite lower left*) extend the range of designs we have encountered so far.

It is hard to say quite what is going on here, and the reader may be forgiven for thinking that research has not progressed a huge amount since the time of the comment below:

> *"If these markings be not Celtic it is difficult to say to what age they belong"*
>
> The Rev. J Mapleton, Dunoon Castle, 1864

Dod Law

Dod Law

Horton Moor

Horton Moor

Dod Law

Doddington

Overlapping Rings & Tailed Cups
Old Bewick, Northumberland

This area of the Northumberland moors lies in the shadow of the Cheviot Hills, and a wealth of rock carvings are found here. The complex carvings on the famous Old Bewick stone (*opposite and below*) show how, in many examples, designs are created by "chasing" lines together. Once again there seems to be a specific purpose or meaning to these markings and the multiple rings, five in this case, intensify the overall design. One of the cups has a forked tail, a significant development from the single line, creating another route to or from the centre. The possible design permutations with so many integral elements must be almost infinite.

Old Bewick, Northumberland

Old Bewick, Northumberland

AREAS & EDGES
fitting the art to the canvas

In some cases it is hard to dismiss the idea that the shape and natural structure of a rock must have influenced and controlled the overall creation of these designs. In the opposite lower right example from Cargill, there is something fascinating about the use of the edge of the stone, and one wonders if this may record some attempt to communicate with natural spirit elements.

Flaws in the surface of a rock are often employed and capitalised upon by petroglyph artists, but, in his 1967 article *Geometry of Cup-and-Ring Marks*, Professor Alexander Thom also suggested that considerable preparation may have been undertaken in smoothing the surface before carving.

Doddington, Northumberland

Letham Grange Stone, Angus

Moonbutts, Cargill, Perthshire

STYLES

Rombald's Moor, Yorks./West Horton, Northumberland

An interesting aspect of this subject is the distinct stylistic differences which exist not only between different sites, but actually within the same area. For instance the Badger Stone on Rombald's Moor (*opposite top*) displays some variations on the cup-and-ring motif while the nearby Idol Stone (*below left*) has significant arrangements of simple cups following the shape of the stone with lines.

The Tree of Life on Snowden Moor (*below right*) has a even more fluid and organic approach with less emphasis on multiple rings, while Northumberland's West Horton Goddess (*opposite bottom*) almost looks like a human or spirit family, with the rings (some quite angular) channelled to allow the tail to pass through. It may be that these differences are due to different artists, but there is also the possibility of styles emerging over a period of time.

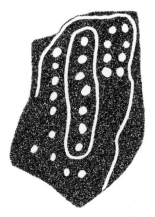

The Idol Stone, Rombald's Moor

The Tree of Life, Rombald's Moor

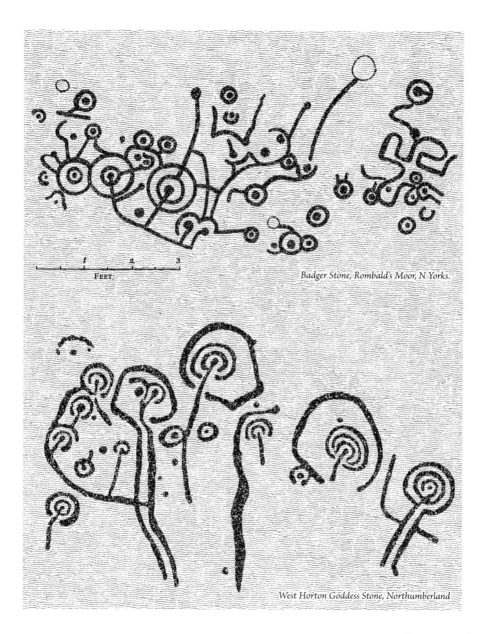

Badger Stone, Rombald's Moor, N.Yorks.

FEET.

West Horton Goddess Stone, Northumberland

SPIRALS
from various sites

The spiral appears regularly in megalithic art at a range of locations, often in combination with other graphic elements.

Regarded in many traditions as symbolic of the divine feminine, the spiral represents the womb, fertility, the serpent, continual change and the passage of time and evolution. Since we know that megalithic peoples were fascinated by the Sun and Moon, it is likely that the spiral, as a development of the circle, may also represent the Sun and the passage of time. Both the Sun and Moon exhibit apparent spiral movement over time, rising and setting in different places every day, and their journey was referred to as "spiralling" by ancient astronomers.

Spirals can have many arms, and the number depicted might have been important to ancient astronomer-artists, possibly representing a number of days or months. In Martin Brennan's reclassification of Neolithic symbols the spiral is one of the primaries, and can be left- or right-handed as well as retrograde (reversing internally). Brennan suggests that the direction of the spiral may indicate "the beginning, growth" (left hand spiral) or "the end, decay" (right hand spiral).

Spirals from Newgrange (1,2 & 4) and Loughcrew (3), Co. Meath, Eire, and Cauldside Burn, Kirkcudbright (5)

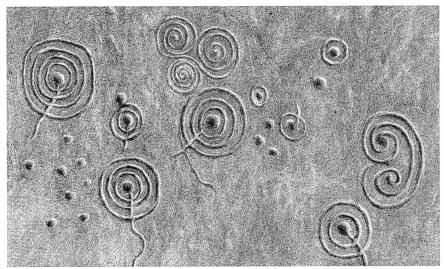

Achnabreck, Argyllshire

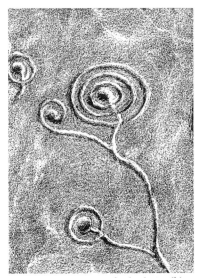

Achnabreck, Argyllshire

Temple Wood Stone Circle, Kilmartin Valley

SHARP ANGLES
triangles, diamonds and zig-zags

The triangle and its associated structures have long been dynamic elements which have been employed by many cultures and religions. In Christianity, Judaism, Tibetan Buddhism, Zen and the more recent Bauhaus, the triangle has been seen and employed as a powerful fundamental element, often associated with a range of qualities and attributed colours. Xenocrates, the Greek philosopher, suggested that the triangle was a symbol for God, and in Christianity it represented the Holy Trinity. It is associated with fire and strength but also with harmony and balance.

The zig-zag could be a reference to, or a symbol for, water but given the complexity of other nearby elements, this may be too simple an explanation of its meaning in this context.

The cist cover from Carnwarth is interesting in that it exhibits differing styles, simultaneously displaying typical ring marks beside the stylised triangular motifs.

These examples show that angular designs were not local to one area or tradition. Whether such simple and universal devices arose spontaneously or through communication between different communities is a matter for debate.

Newgrange, Co. Meath, Eire

Cist Cover, Carnwarth, Lanarkshire

Newgrange, Co. Meath, Eire

Barclodiad y Gawres, Anglesey

Newgrange, Co. Meath, Eire

STARS AND SUNS
Loughcrew & Knowth passage grave, Co. Meath, Eire

The top two drawings on the page opposite resemble and may indeed represent stars. Below, three flower motifs from the same stone are thought to symbolise suns, solar years, or possibly solar year counts (like the 8-year Venus cycle). Or they could possibly represent the Sun at different times of the day or year.

There is an increasing body of research concerning the employment of astronomical alignments by ancient cultures. Evidence is mounting that many of these early communities used the risings and settings of specific heavenly bodies in an intelligent and informed way.

Martin Brennan's drawing *(lower opposite)* is an excellent example of how some of these elements are combined: cups rings, spirals and stars. The diagonal line of cups across the centre seems to suggest a lunar count. The ability to record and apply this kind of information in such an aesthetic manner must have taken great diligence and intelligence.

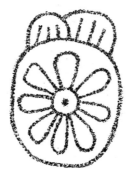

Suns from Cairn T, Loughcrew

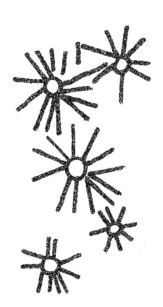

Stars from Dowth

Stars from Knowth

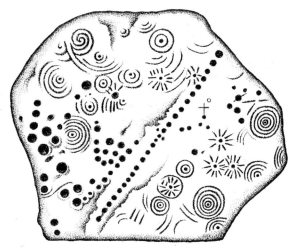

Chamber Roof Slab, near Sess Kilgreen, Co. Tyrone

Irish Megalithic Art
the Boyne valley, Co. Meath

The sheer quantity and quality of megalithic art in the Boyne Valley in Co. Meath emphasises the importance of these sites to those that built them over 5000 years ago.

After extensive research, published in his 1980s book *The Stars and the Stones*, Martin Brennan, who made the drawings of the stones shown here, concluded that most of the art in this area is concerned with astronomical data and alignments. He clearly identified a range of symbols as representing the Sun, the Moon and the passage of time.

Of Kerbstone 15 at Knowth N L Thomas observes:

> *"the stone is a unique statement, an exact 365 day, sixteen month, four-week month, five-day week solar calendar"*

The illustration below is of Knockmany Passage Grave, now enclosed, an example of how rock art was integral to the megalithic culture.

Knockmany, Co. Tyrone

Kerbstone 18 , Newgrange , Co. Meath

Stone S4, Knowth , Co. Meath

SYMBOLS

Loughcrew passage grave, Co. Meath, Eire

The complex mixture of symbols shown at Loughcrew extends the study of rock carvings into an area of greater sophistication in the application and meaning of visual design. The effective minimalism of cup and ring marks, although still visible here, is now accompanied by designs which may have a much more representational root. These could be stars, flowers, leaves and water, but the random arrangements give little clue as to whether the elements are interrelated or simply the outcome of incremental addition. Some of the more representational elements resemble tribal art from Africa or Australia.

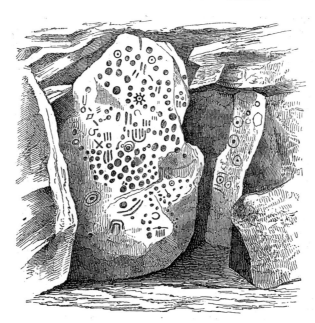

NEWGRANGE PASSAGE TOMB
Newgrange, Co. Meath, Eire

At 9 am on December 21st the dawn rays of the winter solstice sun enter the chamber at Newgrange and illuminate a specific range of pictograms, slowly moving from one to another over 15 minutes as the Sun swings round. A special roof box above the entrance allows the Sun to penetrate right to the back wall.

Two huge kerbstones (*one shown opposite top*) are directly aligned at the front and back of the mound, their central grooves also aligning with the winter solstice.

Built between 3300 and 2900 BC, 500 years before the Great Pyramid of Giza, Newgrange is an amazing construction, beautifully decorated and a testimony to the skills and dedication of those who built it. The conjunction and balance of opposites here, of midsummer and midwinter, Sun and Moon, light and dark, life and death, embody the whole interplay of the forces and energies of regeneration (*lower pictures by Martin Brennan*).

Knowth Burial Chamber, Co. Meath

Kerbstone 1, Newgrange, Co. Meath

Kerbstone 52, Newgrange, Co. Meath

GAVRINIS

Gavrinis Passage Tomb, Morbihan, Brittany

The extensive 3500 BC carvings at Gavrinis display flowing, abstract designs which take account of the shapes of the stones they cover. Are these simply decorative patterns or do they contain clues to some forgotten perception? Perhaps the stones were decorated before being positioned, but they were certainly intended to create a specific impact on the inside of the cairn and to perform a visual function. We may also wonder about the intended viewer, as these structures are primarily houses of the dead—did they have a wider function?

In the end very little is really known about any archaic sculpturings, merely their age. I hope, however, that I have managed to convey something of their mystery, majesty and beauty in these pages.

Gavrinis, Brittany, France

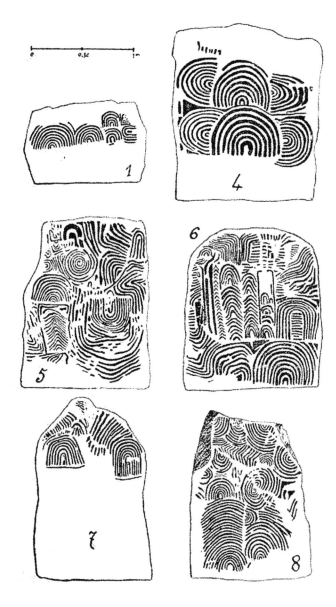

*Gavrinis,
Brittany,
France*

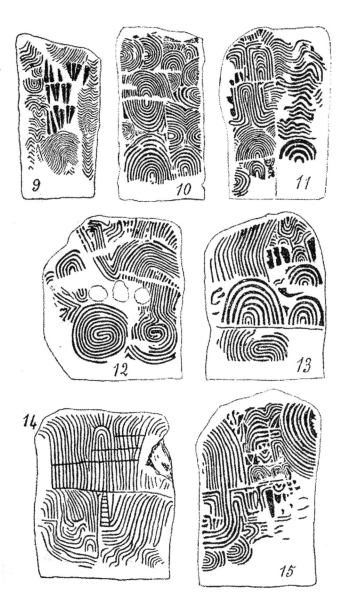

Gavrinis,
Brittany,
France

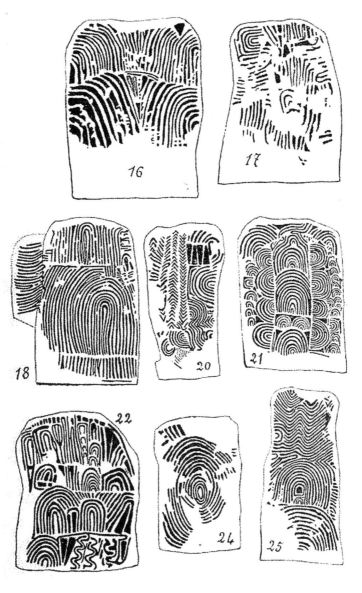

*Gavrinis,
Brittany,
France*

SURVEYS
OF STONE CIRCLES

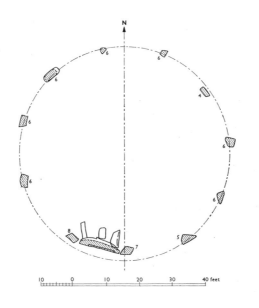

Alexander Thom

Fernacre, Cornwall

50.589952°N, 4.622378°W

Geometry:
type-A flattened

Outlier 351°·5
$h = 5°·2$
$\delta = +43°·9$

N

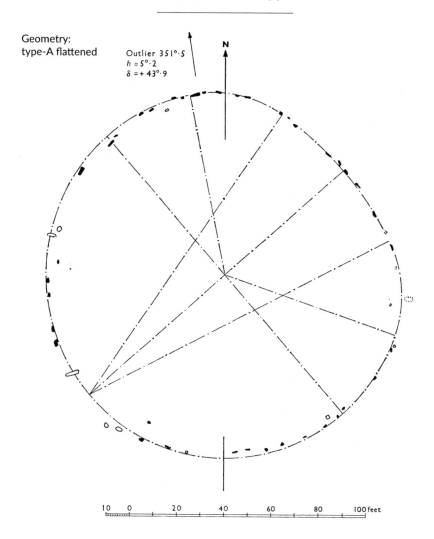

10 0   20   40   60   80   100 feet

Stannon, Cornwall

50.589546°N, 4.650258°W

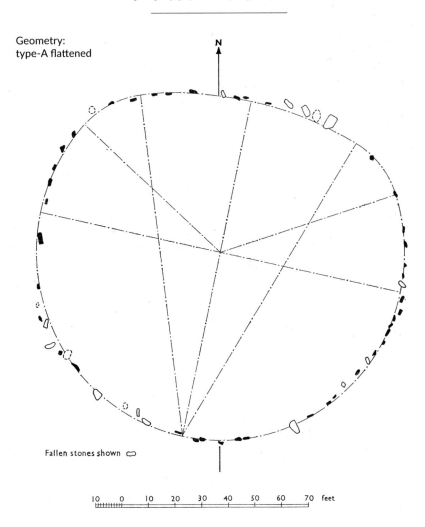

Geometry:
type-A flattened

N

Fallen stones shown ⬭

10 0 10 20 30 40 50 60 70 feet

HOARSTONES, SHROPSHIRE

52.592778°N, 2.999167°W

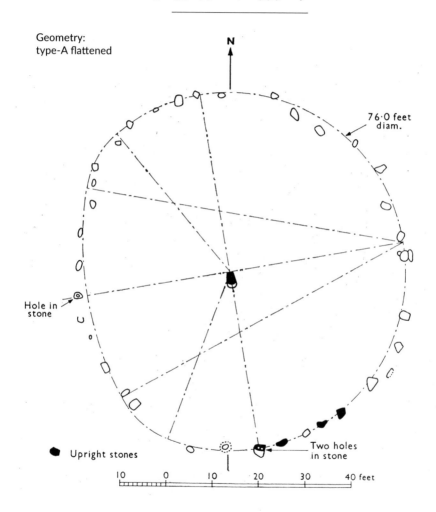

Geometry:
type-A flattened

N

76·0 feet
diam.

Hole in
stone

● Upright stones

Two holes
in stone

10   0   10   20   30   40 feet

BARBROOK, DERBYSHIRE

53.27652°N, 1.583735°W

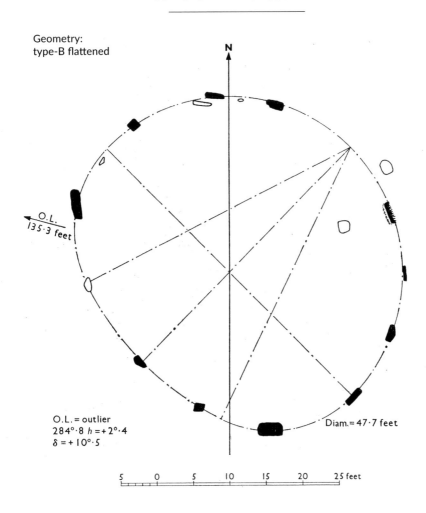

Geometry:
type-B flattened

N

O.L.
135.3 feet

O.L. = outlier
284°·8 h = + 2°·4
δ = + 10°·5

Diam. = 47·7 feet

5   0   5   10   15   20   25 feet

Castlerigg, Cumbria

54.6028°N, 3.0984°W

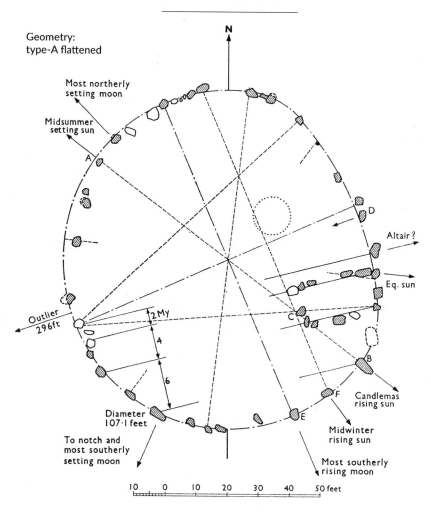

Geometry:
type-A flattened

Most northerly
setting moon

Midsummer
setting sun

A

Outlier
296 ft

2 My

4

6

Diameter
107·1 feet

To notch and
most southerly
setting moon

D

Altair ?

Eq. sun

C

B

F   Candlemas
rising sun

E

Midwinter
rising sun

Most southerly
rising moon

10   0   10   20   30   40   50 feet

Long Meg, Cumbria

54.72794°N, 2.66765°W

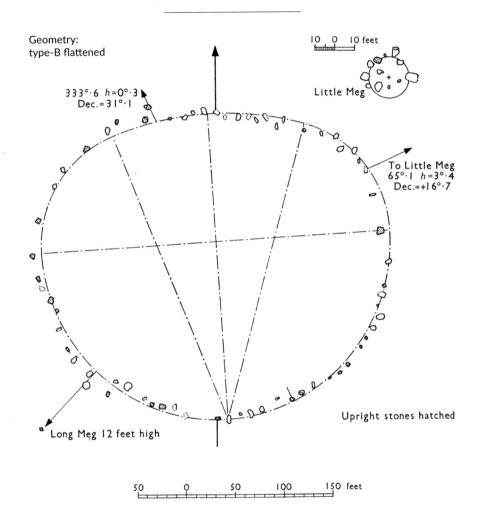

Geometry:
type-B flattened

10 0 10 feet

Little Meg

333°·6 h=0°·3
Dec.=31°·1

To Little Meg
65°·1 h=3°·4
Dec.=+16°·7

Upright stones hatched

Long Meg 12 feet high

50 0 50 100 150 feet

BURNMOOR, CUMBRIA

54.409175°N, 3.274325°W

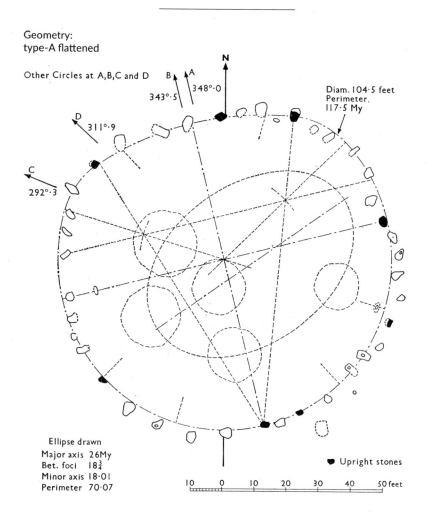

Geometry:
type-A flattened

Other Circles at A,B,C and D

B A 348°·0

343°·5

Diam. 104·5 feet
Perimeter.
117·5 My

D 311°·9

C
292°·3

N

Ellipse drawn
Major axis 26My
Bet. foci 18¾
Minor axis 18·01
Perimeter 70·07

Upright stones

| 10 | 0 | 10 | 20 | 30 | 40 | 50 feet |

CAMBRET MOOR, KIRKCUDBRIGHTSHIRE

55.896389°N, 4.324444°W

Geometry:
type-A flattened

Remains of second circle and
perhaps third on this line
(now removed, 1955)

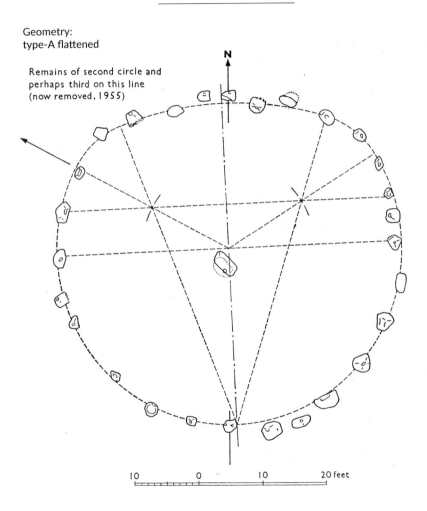

10   0   10   20 feet

CALLANISH I, OUTER HEBRIDES

58.1979°N, 6.7443°W

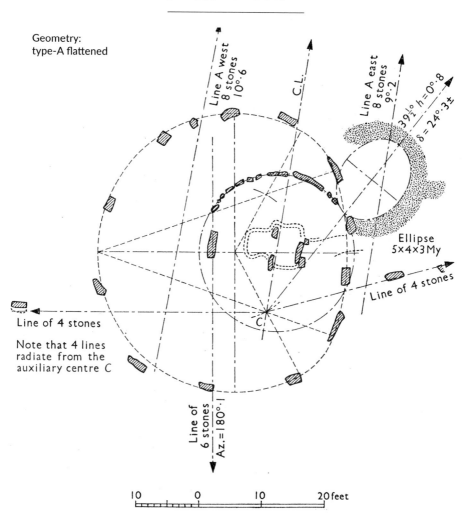

Geometry:
type-A flattened

Line A west
8 stones
10°.6

C.L.

Line A east
8 stones
9°.2

$39\frac{1}{2}°$ h = 0°.8

δ = 24°.3±

Ellipse
5×4×3 My

Line of 4 stones

Line of 4 stones

Note that 4 lines
radiate from the
auxiliary centre C

C

Line of
6 stones
Az. = 180°.1

10   0   10   20 feet

Hirnant, Ceredigion

52.439157°N, 3.835522°W

Geometry:
egg with elliptic end

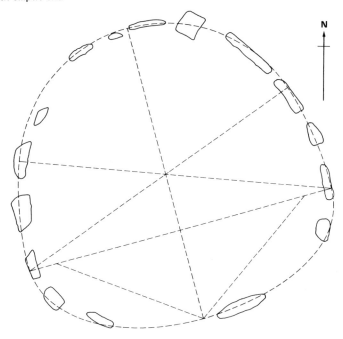

N

Ellipse (MY): $2a=7$, $2b=4$, $2c=5\frac{3}{4}$

$5\frac{3}{4}^2+4^2=49.06$, $7^2=49$

Triangle for arcs (MY): $-a=3\frac{3}{4}$, $b=3\frac{1}{2}$, $c=1\frac{1}{4}$

$3\frac{1}{2}^2+1\frac{1}{4}^2=13.81$, $3\frac{3}{4}^2=14.06$

Perimeter = 21·58 MY

Clava, Highlands

57.472585°N, 4.074469°W

Geometry:
type-I egg

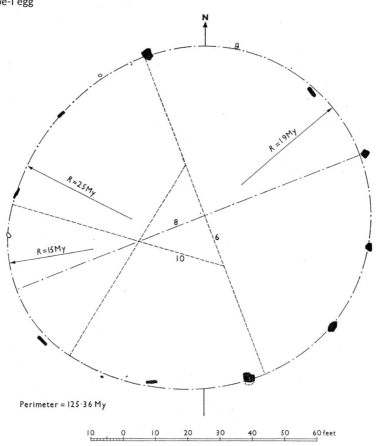

N

R=19My

R=25My

R=15My

8

6

10

Perimeter = 125·36 My

10   0   10   20   30   40   50   60 feet

Druid Temple, Highlands

54.450°N, 4.190°W

Geometry:
type-I egg

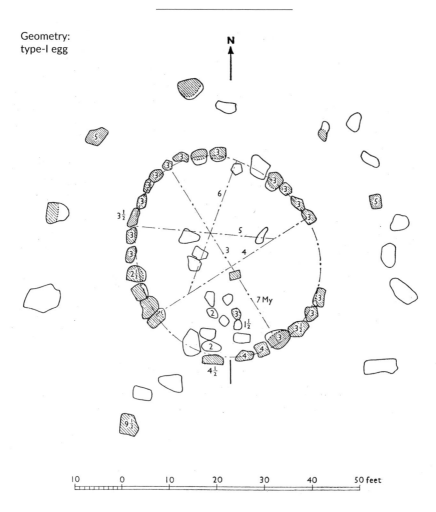

10   0   10   20   30   40   50 feet

ALLAN WATER, SCOTTISH BORDERS

55.3467°N, 2.8350°W

Geometry:
type-I egg

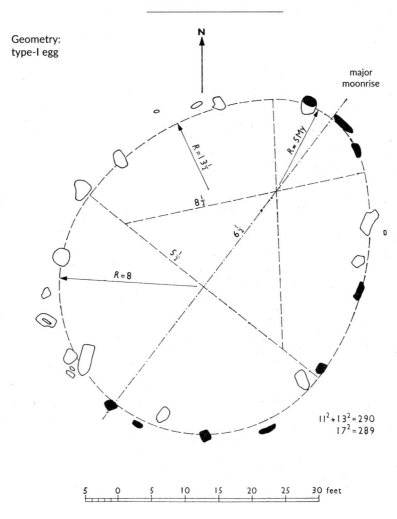

Borrowston Rig, Scottish Borders

55.762151°N, 2.706570°W

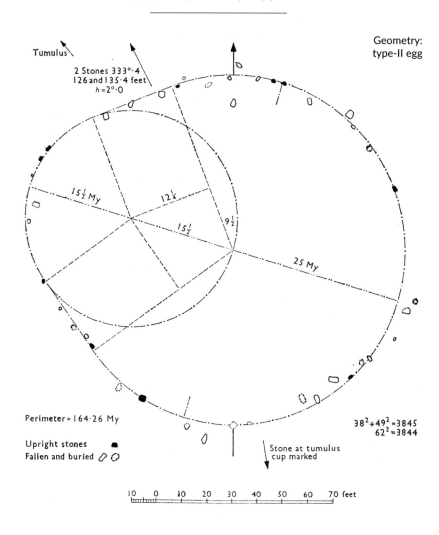

Geometry: type-II egg

Tumulus

2 Stones 333°·4
126 and 135·4 feet
h = 2°·0

$15\frac{1}{2}$ My $12\frac{1}{4}$

$15\frac{1}{2}$ $9\frac{1}{2}$

25 My

Perimeter = 164·26 My

Upright stones ●
Fallen and buried ⬭ ⬭

$38^2 + 49^2 = 3845$
$62^2 = 3844$

Stone at tumulus cup marked

10 0 10 20 30 40 50 60 70 feet

Daviot, Highlands

57.442314°N, 4.122562°W

Geometry:
ellipse

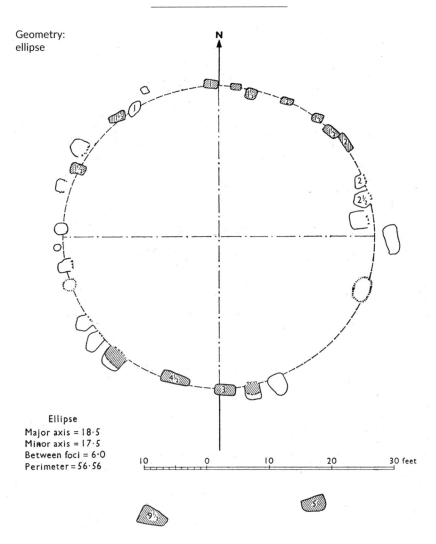

N

Ellipse
Major axis = 18·5
Minor axis = 17·5
Between foci = 6·0
Perimeter = 56·56

10   0   10   20   30 feet

Boat of Garten, Aberdeenshire

57.270584°N, 3.718268°W

Geometry:
ellipse

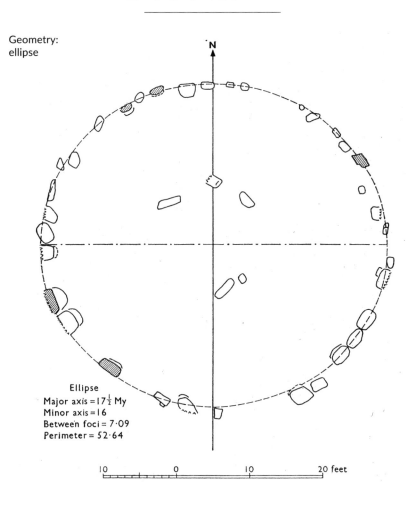

Ellipse
Major axis = $17\frac{1}{2}$ My
Minor axis = 16
Between foci = 7·09
Perimeter = 52·64

10 0 10 20 feet

FORVIE SANDS, ABERDEENSHIRE

57.309188°N, 1.985875°W

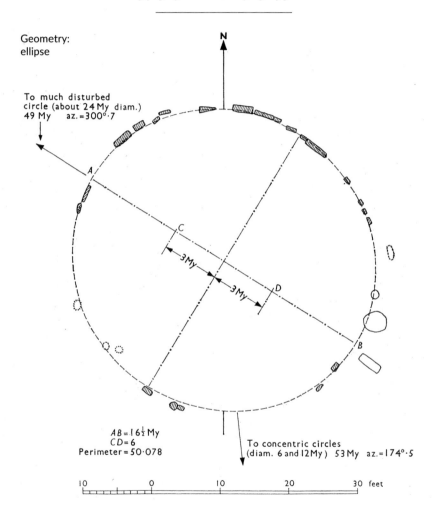

Geometry:
ellipse

N

To much disturbed
circle (about 24 My diam.)
49 My   az.=300°·7

A

C

3 My

3 My

D

B

$AB = 16\frac{1}{2}$ My
$CD = 6$
Perimeter = 50·078

To concentric circles
(diam. 6 and 12My) 53 My az.=174°·5

10   0   10   20   30 feet

POSTBRIDGE, DEVON

50.592860°N, 3.873176°W

Geometry:
ellipse

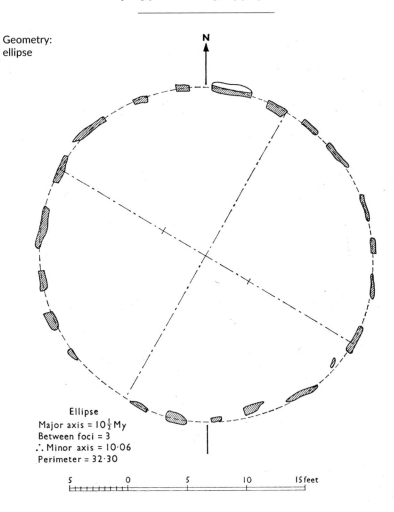

Ellipse
Major axis = $10\frac{1}{2}$ My
Between foci = 3
∴ Minor axis = 10·06
Perimeter = 32·30

MOEL TY UCHAF, MERIONETHSHIRE

52.923618°N, 3.405455°W

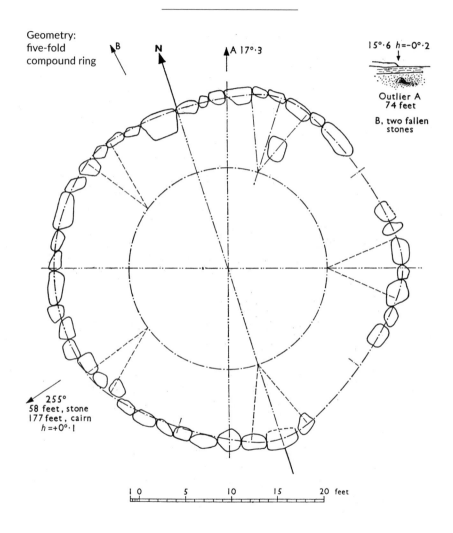

Geometry: five-fold compound ring

B

N

A 17°·3

15°·6 h=−0°·2

Outlier A 74 feet

B, two fallen stones

255°
58 feet, stone
177 feet, cairn
h =+0°·1

1 0   5   10   15   20 feet

Easter Delfour, Highlands

57.153668°N, 3.912555°W

Geometry:
four-fold
compound ring

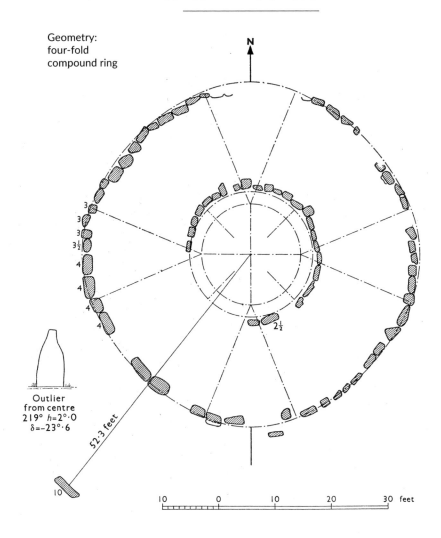

N

3
3
3
3½
4
4
4
4

Outlier
from centre
219° *h*=2°·0
δ=−23°·6

52·3 feet

2½

10

10   0   10   20   30 feet

GEOMETRY OF ROCK CARVINGS

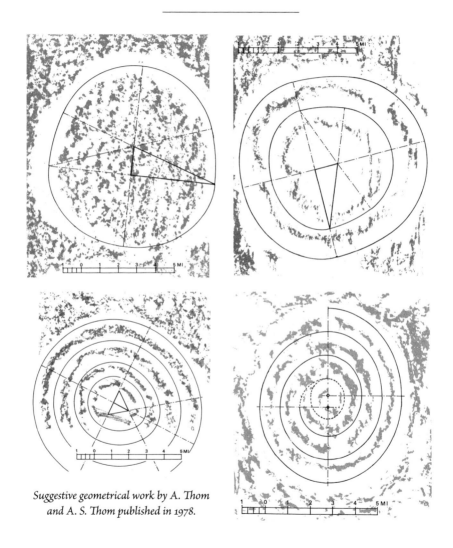

Suggestive geometrical work by A. Thom and A. S. Thom published in 1978.

INDEX

CREDITS

STONE CIRCLES

Thanks to Emmanuel Martin for additional illustrations on pages 7 and 49, Steve Larder for his drawing on page 31, and to John Michell, John Neal, Terence Meaden, Andrew Collins and Stephen Parsons. Many pictures are from 19th century sources, in particular *Rude Stone Monuments* by James Fergusson, 1872. We also borrowed a great number of plates from John Michell's classic compilation of all things megalithic, *Megalithomania*, published by Squeeze Press. Other images are credited where they appear.

CARNAC

Profound thanks to the Association Archéologique Kergal and its founder, the late Helène Fleury, and thanks to the directors and members of L'Association Pour La Connaissance et L'Etude des Megalithes (ACEM). Some images were adpated from *Sun, Moon and Standing Stones*, by John Edwin Wood, Oxford, 1978. Many images are by Blair & Ronalds (see page 72). Images on pages 62 & 97 © Erica Guilane-Nachez via Adobe Stock. Other pictures are credited where they appear.

STONEHENGE

Pictures have been taken from a wide selection of rare antiquarian books and are mostly credited where they appear. The engravings on page 125 are from Inigo Jones' book of 1655, the engraving on page 173 is from William Stukeley's *Stonehenge, A Temple Restored to the British Druids*, 1740, and the picture on page 158 is from Walpoole's late 18th century *Modern British Traveller*. Visit www.robinheath.info for more books by Robin Heath. Further reading: *A Guide to the Stone Circles of Britain, Ireland & Brittany*, by Aubrey Burl, Yale, 1996; *Stonehenge, Mysteries of the Stones and Landscape* by David Souden, English Heritage, 1997.

AVEBURY

Thanks for images and other assistance to the curators of the Alexander Keiller museum, to the Local Studies Unit, Wiltshire Library, Trowbridge, and to Caius Hawkins and Steve Marshall. Images have mainly been taken from William Stukeley's book *Abury, a Temple of the British Druids*, 1743, *Ancient Wiltshire* by Sir Richard Colt Hoare, 1819, plus other titles already mentioned.

STANTON DREW

Thanks to the Arts Librarian at the Reference Library at Bristol Central Library and to Jon King. Please note this is a condensed and abbreviated version of the original book published by Wooden Books.

CALLANISH

Thanks to Dr Alastair Fraser, Elizabeth Ponting, Margaret Curtis, Western Isles Libraries, Chandler's Ford branch of the Hampshire Library Service. Images: National Library of Scotland (283, 293 upper, 303 lower, 315, 317 upper); Nationalmuseet, Copenhagen (288, 289); University of St Andrews Library (303 upper); National Archives, Kew (299 lower, 317 lower); Ordnance Survey (295 upper); Wiltshire Archaeological Society, Devizes (285); Oliver and Boyd (301 lower); Edinburgh University Press (281 lower); Patrick Ashmore and Historic Scotland (281 upper); Gail Kelly (305 lower); Lorraine Tolmie (295 lower). The image on page 275 is taken from a paper by T.A.Wise (1877). Please note this is a condensed and abbreviated version of the original book published by Wooden Books.

ROCK ART

Thanks to Chujé Akong Rinpoché and Sandra Berwald. Further reading: *British Prehistoric Rock Art* by Stan Beckensall (1999). Illustrations are from James Fergusson's *Rude Stone Monuments* (1872), Llewellynn Jewitt's *Grave Mounds and their Contents* (1870), Sir J.Y.Simpson's *Archaic Sculpturings* (1867), George Tate's *Ancient British Sculptured Rocks ...* (1865), Algernon, Duke of Northumberland's *Incised Markings in Stone* (1869), E.T.Cowling's *Rombald's Way* (1946), and Martin Brennan's *The Stars and The Stones* (1984). Other pictures are by the author.

SURVEYS

Surveys of stone circles by Prof. Alexander Thom (and his son Archie) appear throughout this book with the kind permission of Thom's grandson, Eoghann MacColl, with thanks to Robin Heath. Many of them first appeared together in *Megalithic Sites in Britain*, 1967, *Megalithic Lunar Observatories*, 1971, and *Megalithic Remains in Britain and Brittany*, 1978, all published by the Clarendon Press, Oxford. Thom was chair of engineering science at Brasenose College, Oxford. The survey of Hirnant on page 393 was originally made by John Hoyle.

WEB

Wooden Books would like to thank Andy Burnham and all the contributors to *The Megalithic Portal*, www.megalithic.co.uk, a vast global online resource of all things megalithic which can be used to help users find megalithic sites near to their location. It is for this reason that the editors felt it was not necessary to include a gazetteer in this book. The seven individual books which comprise this compendium can be read in full online at www.woodenbooks.com.